Superfoods
RENA PATTEN

First published in 2014 by New Holland Publishers Pty Ltd
London • Sydney • Cape Town • Auckland

The Chandlery Unit 114 50 Westminster Bridge Road London SE1 7QY United Kingdom
1/66 Gibbes Street Chatswood NSW 2067 Australia
Wembley Square First Floor Solan Road Gardens Cape Town 8001 South Africa
218 Lake Road Northcote Auckland New Zealand

www.newhollandpublishers.com

A record of this book is held at the British Library and the National Library of Australia.

ISBN 9781742575063

Managing Director: Fiona Schultz
Publisher: Linda Williams
Project Editor: Jodi De Vantier
Proofreader: Meryl Potter
Designer: Tracy Loughlin
Photography: Sue Stubbs
Food stylist: Tracy Rutherford
Production Director: Olga Dementiev
Printer: Toppan Leefung Printing Ltd (China)

10 9 8 7 6 5 4 3 2 1

Keep up with New Holland Publishers on Facebook
www.facebook.com/NewHollandPublishers

Superfoods

7 essential ingredients for living well

RENA PATTEN

NEW
HOLLAND

DEDICATED TO ALL THE
FARMERS, WHO WORK
TIRELESSLY AND OFTEN UNDER
VERY HARSH AND DIFFICULT
CONDITIONS TO PROVIDE US
WITH OUR FOOD.

Contents

These days we seem to be hearing about the power of 'superfoods' from just about everybody. But what exactly is a superfood? A superfood is supposedly a food that is packed with lots of highly powerful antioxidants, vitamins, minerals, essential fatty acids and other nutrients that are not only supposed to keep you healthy from the inside out but may also help your body ward off diseases. It is a term that is given to foods that are considered to be beneficial to one's health by providing nutrients that naturally nourish the body without any side effects or the use of supplements or drugs.

It is thought that the unusually high amounts of nutrients found in certain foods may be able to help reduce the risk of heart disease, cancer, high blood pressure, high cholesterol and obesity, and rid the body of toxins, as well as instil a feeling of physical and emotional wellbeing.

And in some extreme line of thought it has also been said that regular consumption of superfoods is so beneficial that it may actually help you live longer.

In the past few years, there has been a resurgence of interest in ancient wheat-free grains. Grains that have successfully and nutritionally sustained communities, who have consumed them as part of their staple diet.

Other fruits and vegetables have been re-assessed and are now referred to as superfoods.

As well as labelling certain ingredients as 'superfoods', people have become more aware of what goes into their bodies and seem to have a genuine desire to live a healthier life.

There is a lot more effort put into finding out where the food that is used to fuel the body comes from and what is actually in that food.

This book is an introduction to seven superfoods: some you may be familiar with, others you may not. These seven foods are all packed with large amounts of vitamins, minerals, essential fatty acids and antioxidants, as well as many other nutrients that are considered to be beneficial for a healthier life.

The seven we present here are quinoa, broccoli, kale, amaranth, chia, seaweed and raw cacao. All are considered superfoods with massive amounts of pure and healthy nutrients, and all are considered good for our bodies.

Each chapter is dedicated to one of these superfoods, with many different and easy to prepare recipes using readily available ingredients. These recipes have been created to show some of the varied ways in which each one of these superfood ingredients can be prepared and enjoyed. Many of the recipes use more than one superfood, so you can enjoy even more benefits.

Our list is by no means inclusive of all the nutritious foods that are available to you. It is merely a guide to these specific seven superfoods and the variety of nutritional benefits that each has to offer.

Superfoods are so 'super' because they are natural, pure foods. They aren't processed or packed with additives, enhancers, colours or preservatives. Instead they derive their amazing super-ness from within.

We should be eating a lot less, if any, processed foods and where possible relying on what nature can offer.

Consuming the foods that are good for us should be something that is done on a regular basis as part of a healthy and balanced everyday diet. It should be a normal and natural process to eat healthy food.

It should also be noted, however, that some food, even in their natural state, can interfere with certain life-saving medications and you should seek medical advice before consuming them.

When preparing and cooking any of the recipes in this book, it is important to remember that cooking appliances, especially ovens, are not the same and so will vary in their cooking time. You may need to experiment with your own cooking appliances to work out correct cooking times.

INTRODUCTION

BROCCOLI

Broccoli is a familiar vegetable to many, but you may not know that it is considered to be a major superfood and a very power antioxidant.

Broccoli is a cruciferous vegetable and part of the Brassica family of vegetables. It is very nutritious, with many health benefits. It contains substantial amounts of nutrients considered extremely beneficial for our health, such as vitamins A, C, K, B6, as well as folate, manganese, fibre, folic acid and more.

With its large amount of potassium, broccoli not only helps you to maintain an overall healthier nervous system but also promotes optimal brain function and regular muscle growth.

Broccoli is rich in glucoraphanin, which the body can process into an anti-cancer compound called sulforaphane. This compound eliminates the bacteria *Heliobacter pylori*, which is believed to increase the risk of gastric cancer, from your body. Being rich in indole-3-carbinol means broccoli is a very powerful antioxidant and anti-carcinogen, boosting liver function, and can hinder the growth of breast, prostate and cervical cancers.

Its high fibre content when combined with calcium and magnesium can regulate blood pressure. Broccoli's high level of soluble fibre can aid in reducing cholesterol. Broccoli contains carotenoid lutein that has been found to prevent or slow down the thickening of the arteries in the body, fighting heart disease. It has also been known to help prevent or slow down age-related macular degeneration and cataracts. Broccoli also contains folate and vitamin B6, which may reduce the risk of a heart attack or stroke. Vitamin A in broccoli aids in forming retinal, a light-absorbing molecule.

Calcium and vitamin K, both found in broccoli, are also key players in maintaining bone health and may prevent osteoporosis. Broccoli also contains special phytonutrients that aid in the body's detox process and the neutralisation and elimination of unwanted contaminants.

Precaution

It should also be noted that broccoli contains certain components that may interfere with blood-thinning medications. If you are taking such medications it is advisable to watch your intake of broccoli and not to be excessive with the amount consumed. Consult your physician for advice.

Preparing broccoli

When buying broccoli, select a firm, tightly closed head with dark green florets and no sign of yellowing. Avoid any broccoli that has yellow buds. The stalk should be firm but not tough, and a nice bright colour. Leaves should be crisp and green.

Broccoli should be rinsed under cold running water, and cut into florets for quick and even cooking. There is no need to discard the stems and leaves as they are full of flavour, not to mention vitamins, and add more texture to a dish.

Peel the stems and slice to desired size and cook with the florets. Use the younger, more tender leaves as well.

Broccoli can be eaten raw, steamed, stir-fried or boiled for a very short period of time.

Bring salted water to a rapid boil, throw in the broccoli, cover and as soon as the water comes back to the boil, switch off the heat and leave the broccoli to stand for a few minutes until just tender. Times specified for cooking the broccoli in the recipes should be used as a guide. Broccoli should not be over-cooked; it should be tender yet still crisp.

Also, don't throw out the cooking water. Add it to the dish you are cooking if required.

ARTICHOKE, OLIVE AND BROCCOLI PASTA SALAD

SERVES 4–6

1 lb/500 g broccoli, cut into florets

2 cups cooked small pasta (I used shells)

8 oz/250 g small grape tomatoes

4 oz/125 g black pitted kalamata olives

9 oz/280 g jar artichokes, drained and quartered

2 tablespoons capers

4 scallions/spring onions, sliced

DRESSING

1 small clove garlic, finely grated

⅓ cup extra virgin olive oil

1 tablespoon Dijon mustard

1 tablespoon honey

2 tablespoons red wine vinegar

salt and freshly cracked black pepper

Bring a large saucepan of salted water to the boil, add the broccoli and cook for 3-4 minutes until just tender but still a little firm.

Drain and place into a bowl of iced water to stop the cooking process and for the broccoli to retain that vibrant green colour.

When completely cooled, drain well and place into a large bowl with the pasta, tomatoes, olives, artichokes, capers and scallions. Gently toss together to combine.

Whisk all the dressing ingredients together, pour over the salad and toss. Taste and adjust seasoning as needed.

This salad is best if prepared at least 2-3 hours in advance so as to allow all the flavours to combine and for the pasta and broccoli to absorb the dressing.

NOTE: YOU CAN DOUBLE THE QUANTITY OF INGREDIENTS TO MAKE A REALLY BIG SALAD IF FEEDING A CROWD; IT KEEPS REALLY WELL AND IMPROVES WITH AGE. ANY LEFTOVERS ARE GREAT FOR WORK LUNCHES.

BACON AND BROCCOLI TORTILLA

SERVES 4

14 oz/400 g broccoli, cut into
    small florets
⅓ cup extra virgin olive oil
3 medium potatoes, peeled
    and cubed
2 medium onions, halved and
    finely sliced
3 rashers bacon, rind removed,
    and chopped
2 cloves garlic, finely chopped
8 eggs
½ teaspoon paprika
2 tablespoons chopped flat-leaf
    parsley
salt and freshly ground black
    pepper

Bring a medium-sized saucepan of salted water to the boil over high heat. Toss in the broccoli and cook for 3-4 minutes, until just tender. Drain and place into a bowl of iced water to stop the cooking process.

Heat the oil in a medium-sized, non-stick frying pan and cook the potatoes on medium heat, turning often until tender and golden.

Using a slotted spoon, remove the potatoes from the pan and transfer to another dish.

Remove most of the oil from the pan and set aside in case you need more when cooking the other ingredients.

Heat the oil that is left in the pan until hot, add the onion and cook until soft, add the bacon and continue cooking until the onions and bacon are slightly browned.

Stir in the garlic and cook for about 1 minute. Return the potatoes to the pan and combine with the onion and bacon. Arrange the well-drained broccoli over the top.

Whisk the eggs with the paprika and parsley, season with salt and pepper then pour over the vegetables. Swirl the pan to evenly distribute the eggs and cook over a gentle heat until the egg is set.

Place the pan under a preheated medium-hot grill and finish cooking the tortilla until golden and completely set on the top.

Using a spatula, loosen the tortilla from the side of the pan and carefully slide onto a serving dish. Cut into thick wedges.

Serve the tortilla hot or at room temperature.

NOTE: THIS TORTILLA IS GREAT TO TAKE ON PICNICS AS IT CAN BE EATEN COLD. FOR A VEGETARIAN OPTION, LEAVE OUT THE BACON.

BEEF STIR-FRY WITH GINGER AND BROCCOLI

SERVES 4

Mix together the stock, flour, soy sauce and sugar, stir until the flour and sugar have dissolved. Set aside.

Heat olive oil and sesame oil in a wok or a large deep frying pan over high heat until very hot.

Add the steak and stir-fry in batches for about 3-4 minutes or until browned and cooked. Remove each batch from the pan, set aside and keep warm.

After all the meat has been cooked add a little more oil to the wok if necessary, heat on high heat until hot again and add the ginger, garlic and chilli and toss for about 1-2 minutes until fragrant.

Give the stock mixture a quick stir then pour into the wok. Stir in the broccoli and simmer for about 5 minutes until the broccoli is tender but still a little crisp and the sauce has thickened. Stir the wok regularly.

Return the meat to the wok and toss until heated through.

Serve with rice.

1½ cups beef stock
1 generous tablespoon cornflour/cornstarch
3 tablespoons tamari soy sauce
1 teaspoon brown sugar
2 tablespoons olive oil or rice bran oil
1 teaspoon sesame oil
21 oz/600 g rump steak, cut into thin strips
1 knob ginger (about 1½ in/4 cm), sliced
3 cloves garlic, sliced
1 long red chilli, sliced
24 oz/750 g fresh broccoli, cut into florets

NOTE: IF USING STORE-BOUGHT STOCK YOU MAY WANT TO USE ONE THAT IS LOW IN SALT AS THE SOY SAUCE CAN ALSO BE QUITE SALTY.

BROCCOLI WITH BREADCRUMBS AND GARLIC

SERVES 4

24 oz/750 g broccoli, cut into small florets
1/4 cup extra virgin olive oil
4 cloves garlic, sliced
4 scallions/spring onions, sliced
1/2 -1 teaspoon chilli flakes
2 cups fresh breadcrumbs
salt
freshly cracked black pepper (optional)
juice of 1/2 -1 lemon

Bring a large saucepan of salted water to the boil over high heat. Add the broccoli and cook until tender but still crisp, about 3-4 minutes maximum. Remove from the heat and drain well

Heat the oil in a large frying pan and cook garlic, scallions and chilli for 2-3 minutes until soft and just starting to change colour.

Add the breadcrumbs to the garlic and scallions and cook 2-3 minutes until they start to toast. Keep tossing the pan so the breadcrumbs don't burn. Add a little extra oil if mixture seems dry as you want the breadcrumbs to cook and take on some colour.

Add the broccoli and toss really well to combine. Season with salt and pepper, and continue cooking and tossing until the broccoli is heated through.

Squeeze as much lemon juice over the broccoli as you like and serve with an extra drizzle of extra virgin olive oil.

NOTE: ANY TYPE OF FRESH BREADCRUMBS WORKS WELL IN THIS DISH. YOU CAN ALSO USE BROCCOLINI IF YOU PREFER. FOR A GLUTEN-/WHEAT-FREE OPTION YOU CAN USE QUINOA FLAKES INSTEAD OF THE BREADCRUMBS. USE LESS QUINOA FLAKES THAN SPECIFIED IN THE RECIPE AND YOU WILL HAVE TO COOK THE FLAKES A LITTLE LONGER AS WELL.

BROCCOLI FRITTERS

MAKES ABOUT 10–12 FRITTERS

Bring a medium-sized saucepan of salted water to the boil. Cut the broccoli into small florets and cook in the salted water until tender.

Drain well and chop the broccoli into very small pieces and set aside.

Whisk the eggs then stir in the broccoli, scallions, parsley, cilantro, garlic, cumin, salt and pepper. Add the flour and mix to combine.

Heat the oil in a frying pan until medium-hot, drop spoonfuls of the broccoli mixture into the oil and cook until golden on both sides. This is best done in batches.

Remove the fritters from the pan with a slotted spoon and drain on kitchen paper towels

Serve with Greek yoghurt.

15 oz/450 g broccoli, cut into florets
3 extra large eggs, lightly beaten
3 scallions/spring onions, finely sliced
2 tablespoons finely chopped flat-leaf parsley
2 tablespoons finely chopped cilantro/coriander
2 cloves garlic, finely grated
1 teaspoon ground cumin (generous teaspoon)
salt and freshly ground black pepper
½ cup self-raising flour
olive oil, for shallow frying
unsweetened Greek yoghurt, for serving

NOTE: FOR A GLUTEN-FREE ALTERNATIVE YOU CAN USE QUINOA FLOUR INSTEAD OF WHEATEN FLOUR. THESE FRITTERS ARE A GOOD WAY TO USE UP ANY LEFTOVER COOKED BROCCOLI AND I FIND THEY ARE A GREAT WAY TO GET KIDS TO EAT BROCCOLI AS THEY USUALLY LOVE THEM.

BROCCOLI

23

BROCCOLI, BEETROOT AND FETA SALAD

SERVES 4

1 lb/500 g fresh beetroot
24 oz/750 g broccoli, cut into
  small florets
4 scallions/spring onions, sliced
4 oz/125 g feta cheese

DRESSING

4 tablespoons extra virgin
  olive oil
2 teaspoons red wine vinegar
1 tablespoon horseradish cream
1 tablespoon mayonnaise
1 small clove garlic, very finely
  grated
salt and freshly cracked black
  pepper

Preheat the oven to 400°F/200°C. Scrub the beetroot and leave about 1 in/2 cm of the stalk intact, brush with a little extra virgin olive and roast in the oven with the skin on for 20-30 minutes until tender.

Cool then peel and cut into cubes.

In the meantime, bring a large saucepan of salted water to the boil, add the broccoli and cook for 2-3 minutes, then rinse and place into a bowl of iced water to stop the cooking process. Drain well.

Place the beetroot, broccoli, scallions and half the feta into a bowl and gently toss. Transfer to a serving dish and crumble the remaining feta on top.

Serve the salad with the dressing separately in a jug so that everyone can help themselves.

To make the dressing, whisk all of the ingredients together and place into a small serving jug or bowl.

NOTE: YOU MAY WISH TO USE GLOVES WHILE SCRUBBING AND PEELING THE BEETROOT TO AVOID STAINS. YOU CAN TOSS THE DRESSING THROUGH THE SALAD IF YOU PREFER. I PREFER NOT TO AND TO SERVE IT SEPARATELY AS THE BEETROOT TENDS TO 'BLEED' THROUGH THE SALAD AS SOON AS THE DRESSING IS ADDED.

BROCCOLI WITH BACON, GARLIC AND ALMONDS

SERVES 6

Dry roast the almonds in a small non-stick frying pan until golden. Keep tossing them regularly so they do not burn, remove from pan and set aside.

Bring a large saucepan of salted water to the boil over high heat. Toss in the broccoli and cook for about 2–3 minutes until just tender and still bright green.

Remove from the heat and drain well but reserve a little of the water.

Heat the oil in a large frying pan and cook the bacon until crisp. Add the garlic and chilli and cook for about 1 minute until fragrant, stirring constantly so that the garlic does not burn.

Add the almonds and broccoli, season with salt and pepper to taste and toss until the broccoli is well combined with the other ingredients. Add a splash of the reserved broccoli water if pan dries out too much.

7 oz/200 g whole raw almond kernels
2 lb 4 oz/1 kg broccoli, cut into small florets
3 tablespoons extra virgin olive oil
3 rashers bacon, rind removed and cut into strips
4 cloves garlic, sliced
1–2 red chillies, de-seeded and sliced
salt
freshly cracked black pepper

NOTE: YOU CAN USE BROCCOLINI IN THIS DISH INSTEAD OF THE STANDARD BROCCOLI. THIS IS A REALLY NICE DISH SERVED AS A MAIN MEAL WITH STEAMED RICE OR AS A SIDE DISH. FOR A VEGETARIAN OPTION, LEAVE OUT THE BACON.

BROCCOLI, LENTIL AND TOMATO SALAD

SERVES 6–8

Cut the broccoli into small florets, and peel and thinly slice the stalks.

Bring a large saucepan of salted water to the boil, add the broccoli and cook for 3-4 minutes until just tender.

Drain and place into a bowl of iced water to stop the cooking process and retain the vibrant green colour.

Place the lentils into a bowl with the broccoli, red onion, tomatoes and scallions. Tomatoes can be left whole or halved.

Mix together the lime juice, olive oil, cumin, salt and pepper.

Pour dressing over the salad and toss well to combine. Adjust the amount of dressing and seasoning to suit your taste if necessary.

24 oz/750 g broccoli
2 x 14 oz/400 g cans brown lentils, rinsed and drained
1 small red onion, finely chopped
9 oz/250 g small grape or cherry tomatoes
3 scallions/spring onions
juice of 1-1½ limes
4 tablespoons extra virgin olive oil
½ teaspoon ground cumin
salt and freshly cracked black pepper

NOTE: THIS IS ONE OF MY FAVOURITE DISHES. IT CAN BE A MEAL ON ITS OWN OR A SALAD WITH MEAT, CHICKEN OR FISH. I SOMETIMES ADD A CAN OF GOOD QUALITY TUNA FOR A COMPLETE MEAL.

BROCCOLI, TOMATO, RICOTTA AND OLIVE BAKE

SERVES 4

24 oz/750 g broccoli
1½ cups passata tomato sauce
2 cloves garlic, sliced
2 tablespoons chopped chives
½ -1 teaspoon dried oregano
   leaves
½ -1 teaspoon fennel seeds
2 tablespoons extra virgin
   olive oil
salt and freshly cracked black
   pepper
½ cup pitted kalamata black
   olives
7 oz/200 g ricotta cheese
shaved parmesan cheese

Preheat the oven to 400°F/200°C.

Cut the broccoli into florets, and peel and thinly slice the more tender part of the stems.

Bring a large saucepan of salted water to the boil, add the broccoli and cook for 5 minutes only, drain then rinse under cold water then drain again.

Mix the tomato sauce with the garlic, chives, oregano, fennel seeds and oil, and season with salt and pepper to taste.

Place the broccoli and olives into a baking dish and crumble some of the ricotta over the top.

Pour the tomato mixture over the broccoli and crumble the remaining ricotta on top.

Finish off with some shaved parmesan and bake for about 20-25 minutes until slightly golden on top.

NOTE: THIS MAKES A LOVELY VEGETABLE SIDE DISH WITH MEAT OR FISH AND IS JUST AS GOOD ON ITS OWN AS A VEGETARIAN MAIN SERVED WITH CRUSTY BREAD.

CHICKEN, CASHEW AND BROCCOLI STIR-FRY

Place the chicken into a bowl with the garlic and kecap manis. Mix well and marinate for 10-15 minutes.

Heat oils in a wok or large, deep-sided frying pan until hot, add the chicken in two batches and stir-fry over high heat for 3-4 minutes until golden, remove from the pan and set aside.

Add a little more oil to the wok if necessary then add the chilli, broccoli and capsicum and stir-fry for about 4-5 minutes or until vegetables are tender but still crisp. Add the shallots and cashews and stir-fry for about 2 minutes until they take on some colour.

Mix together the soy sauce, shao-xing wine, water and the cornflour, add to the vegetables and stir-fry until the sauce thickens.

Return the chicken to the pan and stir-fry until well combined and the chicken has heated through.

24 oz/750 g chicken breast fillets, trimmed and sliced thinly
2 cloves garlic, finely chopped
1½ tablespoons kecap manis
1-2 tablespoons oil
½ teaspoon sesame oil
1 green chilli, sliced
1 lb/500 g broccoli, cut into florets
1 red bell pepper/capsicum, diced
6 scallions/spring onions, thickly sliced diagonally
4 oz/125 g raw cashews
2 tablespoons soy sauce
2 tablespoons shao-xing wine
2 tablespoons water
1 heaped teaspoon cornflour/cornstarch

NOTE: SERVE WITH STEAMED RICE OR WITH SOME NOODLES STIRRED THROUGH.

BROCCOLI, OLIVE AND FETA CHEESE FRITTATA

SERVES 4—6

1 lb/500 g broccoli, cut into small florets
1 large leek
2 tablespoons extra virgin olive oil
1-2 cloves garlic, finely chopped
8 extra large eggs
freshly ground black pepper
salt
½ cup pitted kalamata olives
4 oz/125 g feta cheese
3 tablespoons chopped chives

Bring a large saucepan of salted water to the boil, add the broccoli and cook for 3-4 minutes or until tender. Drain and set aside.

Wash leek thoroughly and slice very thinly. Heat oil in a medium-sized frying pan and cook leek until it is soft and golden.

Stir in the garlic, cook for a few seconds until fragrant then add the broccoli and cook until the broccoli is heated through.

In the meantime, whisk the eggs with the pepper and a little salt, keeping in mind that both the feta and olives can be quite salty.

Pour the egg mixture over the broccoli and swirl the pan to evenly distribute the egg mixture.

Scatter the olives over the broccoli, crumble the feta over the top then sprinkle with the chives.

Cook the frittata on low-medium heat until it is set but still runny on the top.

Place the frying pan under a preheated grill and cook on medium heat until the frittata is set and golden.

Allow to rest for 2-3 minutes before loosening with a spatula and sliding on to a serving dish.

NOTE: CAN BE SERVED HOT, WARM OR COLD. AN EASIER WAY TO CLEAN LEEKS IS TO SLICE THE LEEK FIRST AND WASH THE SLICED LEEK IN A BOWL OF WATER.

CREAMY BROCCOLI AND CELERIAC SOUP

SERVES 6

2 tablespoons extra virgin olive
   oil
1 large onion, chopped
2 cloves garlic, chopped
24 oz/750 g celeriac, peeled
   and chopped
2 lb 4 oz/1 kg broccoli, cut into
   florets
1 tablespoon grated fresh
   turmeric
2 bay leaves
1 tablespoon chopped fresh
   rosemary
8 cups hot chicken or
   vegetable stock
salt and freshly cracked black
   pepper
1/4 -1/3 cup cream, to serve
   (optional)

GARNISH
1 tablespoon extra virgin olive
   oil
2 large sprigs rosemary
salt

Heat oil in a large saucepan and sauté the onion until soft and translucent, take care not to burn it.

Stir in the garlic and sauté for a further 30 seconds until fragrant.

Add the celeriac, broccoli, turmeric, bay leaves and rosemary. Pour in the stock and season with salt and pepper.

Bring to the boil, reduce the heat, cover and simmer for 15-20 minutes until the vegetables are tender.

Remove the bay leaves and purée the soup. Return to the heat and cook for a further 5 minutes on low heat until heated through. Check and adjust the seasoning if necessary.

To make the garnish, heat the oil in a small frying pan, run your fingers down the rosemary stalks to remove the leaves and add to the hot oil.

Quickly fry until they start to change colour then remove from the pan and drain on kitchen paper.

Serve the soup garnished with a dollop of cream, a scattering of rosemary garnish and a good grind of black pepper.

NOTE: FRESH TURMERIC IS AVAILABLE AT MOST GREENGROCERS AND IS CONSIDERED TO BE A NATURAL ANTI-INFLAMMATORY. IT IS REALLY WORTH USING AS IT ADDS A LOVELY TASTE AND NATURAL COLOUR TO THE DISH. IF YOU CANNOT FIND IT USE 1 TEASPOON OF GROUND TURMERIC INSTEAD.

GRILLED BROCCOLI, SHRIMP AND FENNEL SALAD

Cut the broccoli into florets and peel and slice some of the more tender stems. Bring a large saucepan of salted water to the boil, add the broccoli and cook for 2–3 minutes only, then drain and place into a bowl of iced water to stop the cooking process. Drain well and pat dry.

Remove and discard any tough outer leaves from the fennel and cut in half. Remove and discard the hard core of the fennel and slice the fennel bulb.

Peel and de-vein the prawns, leaving the tail intact.

Lightly salt the broccoli, fennel and prawns, and coat with a little extra virgin olive oil. Either grill under a hot griller or on a griddle pan or barbecue until the vegetables are tender and lightly charred, and the prawns are cooked.

Place into a bowl and toss through the dressing. Transfer onto a serving platter.

To make the dressing: heat the oil over a gentle heat until hot but not smoking hot.

Remove from the heat and toss in the garlic and chilli, swirl the pan so that the garlic and chilli gently cook on the residual heat of the pan and become fragrant. Remove from the pan and slightly cool, then stir in the chives, parsley, lemon juice to taste and season with salt and pepper.

2 lb 4 oz/1 kg broccoli
1 head fennel
1 lb/500 g green shrimp/
  prawns
extra virgin olive oil

DRESSING
⅓ cup extra virgin olive oil
3 cloves garlic, sliced
1–2 long red chillies, de-seeded
  and chopped
2 tablespoons chopped chives
2 tablespoons finely chopped
  flat-leaf parsley
juice of 1–2 lemons
salt and freshly cracked black
  pepper

NOTE: THIS IS A BEAUTIFUL SALAD THAT LOOKS STUNNING. IT IS IDEAL FOR WHEN YOU WANT TO SERVE SOMETHING THAT LITTLE BIT EXTRA SPECIAL.

PASTA WITH BROCCOLI

SERVES 4–6

1 lb/500 g pasta such as
penne or orecchiette
2 lb 4 oz/1 kg broccoli, cut into
florets
¼ cup extra virgin olive oil
4-5 cloves garlic, sliced
½ -1 teaspoon dried chilli flakes
4-5 anchovy fillets, finely
chopped (optional)
½ cup grated parmesan or
romano cheese
salt and freshly cracked black
pepper

Cook the pasta and broccoli together in a large saucepan of salted boiling water until the pasta is cooked to al dente. At this point the broccoli will be a lot more tender than you would normally have it, but you need that for this recipe.

Reserve 1 cup of the pasta water then drain the pasta and broccoli.

Heat the oil in a large, deep, frying pan and cook the garlic until fragrant and it just starts to slightly change colour.

Add the chilli and anchovies, and cook for 1-2 minutes until the anchovies dissolve.

Add the pasta and broccoli to the pan and coat completely with the garlic and the chilli.

Add as much of the reserved pasta water as is necessary to create a sauce and the pasta is not dry.

Stir in the cheese, and season with salt and pepper to taste if you feel more seasoning is necessary. Cook for 2-3 minutes, stirring regularly so that the broccoli breaks up even more, the cheese melts and you have a creamy pasta dish.

Drizzle a little extra virgin olive oil over the pasta and serve with extra grated cheese on top.

NOTE: THE ANCHOVIES ARE REALLY VERY SUBTLE IN THIS DISH, AS ONCE THEY DISSOLVE YOU CANNOT REALLY TASTE THEM AT ALL. THEY DO, HOWEVER, ADD THAT LITTLE SOMETHING EXTRA.

LEEK AND BROCCOLI SOUP WITH PARMESAN CHEESE

SERVES 4–6

Separate the broccoli heads into small florets, and peel and thinly slice the more tender stems.

Trim the leeks and thoroughly wash until all the grit and dirt is removed then chop into thin slices.

Heat the oil and melt the butter in a large saucepan and sauté the leeks until soft.

Stir in the garlic and cook for about 1 minute until fragrant. Add the broccoli stems and florets and stir until well combined.

Pour in the stock and season with a little salt (keep in mind the stock and cheese are salty) and a good grind of pepper. Bring to the boil, reduce the heat, cover and simmer for 15-20 minutes until the broccoli is tender.

Remove from the heat and purée either in a blender or with a stick blender.

Stir in the parmesan cheese then check and adjust the seasoning.

Serve garnished with croutons and shavings of parmesan cheese.

2 lb 4 oz/1 kg broccoli
2 leeks
2 tablespoons extra virgin olive oil
1 tablespoon butter (optional)
2-3 cloves garlic, chopped
8 cups chicken or vegetable stock
salt and freshly cracked black pepper
½ cup grated parmesan cheese
croutons, to serve
shaved parmesan, for garnish

NOTE: AS AN ALTERNATIVE THIS SOUP CAN BE MADE USING CHORIZO SAUSAGE OR BACON. COOK THE SLICED CHORIZO OR BACON AT THE BEGINNING UNTIL GOLDEN. REMOVE FROM THE PAN, SET ASIDE AND CONTINUE PREPARING THE SOUP AS PER THE RECIPE. STIR IN THE CHORIZO OR BACON AFTER THE SOUP HAS BEEN BLENDED.

SAUTÉED BROCCOLI AND KALE WITH PINE NUTS AND RAISINS

Heat the oil in a large deep frying pan and sauté the garlic and chillies until soft and fragrant. Keep an eye on them as you don't want the garlic to burn.

Thoroughly wash the kale, discard the stalks and finely shred the leaves and the more tender upper parts of the stalks.

Cut the broccoli into small florets and add to the pan with the kale, pine nuts and raisins and toss until the vegetables are well coated in the oil and start to soften.

Pour in the wine and water, season to taste and keep tossing until most of the liquid has evaporated, the kale collapses and broccoli becomes tender but still has a slight crispness to it.

Stir in the vinegar and toss to combine.

2-3 tablespoons extra virgin olive oil
4 cloves garlic, sliced
1-2 red chillies, de-seeded and sliced
1 bunch kale
1 lb/500 g broccoli
3 oz/90 g pine nuts
3/4 cup golden raisins/sultanas
1/2 cup white wine
1/4 cup water
salt and freshly cracked pepper
1-2 tablespoons balsamic vinegar

NOTE: SERVE AS A SIDE DISH TO MEAT, CHICKEN OR FISH OR WITH BOILED RICE OR QUINOA AS A MAIN MEAL. ALWAYS START WITH THE LESSER QUANTITY OF VINEGAR AND INCREASE THE AMOUNT TO SUIT YOUR TASTE.

KALE

This frilly leafed, highly nutritional green vegetable has really surged in popularity of late as the health benefits associated with kale become more obvious and widespread.

People are becoming very aware of how beneficial it is to include kale regularly in their diet. A member of the cabbage genus, *Brassica*, kale can be described as a nutritional powerhouse vegetable, which has significant health benefits and is rich in nutrients. It is also delicious and can be adapted to use in so many dishes.

Kale is a Scottish name and this vegetable goes back in time even before the rounded cabbage and spinach as we know them today were established. In the Middle Ages, it was one of the main green vegetables used across most parts of Europe. It was also widely used in Scotland where kale fields grew in abundance.

The main health benefits of kale are linked to the high concentration of antioxidants, phytonutrients and vitamins A, C and K. Kale is a natural antioxidant and anti-inflammatory. It is also a natural detoxifier, keeping your body healthy.

Kale is also a rich source of other minerals, such as calcium, copper, iron, potassium, protein, folate, manganese, phosphorous and more.

Vitamin K promotes bone formation and strengthening, and normal healthy blood clotting. It can help limit damage to brain cells and can aid in the prevention of calcium build-up in the arteries.

Kale is thought to help reduce high blood cholesterol levels and reduce the risk of heart disease due to the high fibre content, which tends to bind all the bile acids together.

Beta-carotene, one of the main antioxidants found in kale, is thought by many nutritional experts to be of great benefit to contributing in the fight against cancer by blocking and destroying cancer cell growth.

Kale has high concentrations of carotenoids and flavonoids which are antioxidants that can help our bodies expel free radicals and help protect us in the fight against cancer. It can help with weight control as it is fat-free, high in fibre, cholesterol-free and low in calories.

It is believed that kale has a higher iron content than beef. Iron is needed to produce haemoglobin, which is essential for transporting oxygen in the blood, proper liver function and for general good health.

Kale is also very high in calcium, which is helpful in preventing bone loss.

The sulphur in the kale and its high fibre content helps detoxify the body and keep the liver healthy.

Kale is a great anti-inflammatory food as it is rich in omega-3 fatty acids, essential in reducing inflammation in the body and boosting brain function.

Precaution

It should also be noted that kale comes with certain components that may interfere with blood-thinning medications. If you are taking such medications it is advisable to watch your intake of kale and not to be excessive with the amount consumed and should consult your doctor for advice before doing so.

Varieties of kale

The most common type of kale and the one most readily available is curly kale. The second most common is the lucinato kale also known as the italian cavolo nero, tuscan kale or dinosaur kale. Then there is the more recently cultivated ornamental kale, which can be white, purple or green.

When buying kale, look for bunches that have firm and thick deep green leaves. Avoid bunches with yellow leaves or that look soft and about to wilt.

Preparation

The size of the bunches varies, but a large bunch usually has eight-ten large leaves.

The best way to prepare kale is to thoroughly wash the kale then remove the thick, tough stalks. Chop the leaves and use as per the recipe. You can also use the upper, more tender, parts of the stalk, which is something that I normally do in most of my recipes. They should be chopped finely before use.

A little tip: when chopping kale it is always a good idea to use a large chopping board or you will have kale going everywhere.

CHICKEN, KALE AND AMARANTH SOUP

SERVES 4—6

1 large onion, chopped
2 ripe tomatoes, skinned and
  chopped
1 clove garlic
1 large bunch or 2 small
  bunches kale, stalks removed
  and roughly chopped
8 cups hot chicken stock
4 chicken thigh cutlets
½ cup amaranth
salt and freshly ground black
  pepper
zest and juice of 1 lemon, to
  serve
pinch of red chilli flakes

SPICE MIX
2-3 tablespoons extra virgin
  olive oil
3 cloves garlic, finely grated
1 teaspoon ground coriander
2 teaspoons ground cumin

Place the onion, tomatoes, garlic and kale into a food processor and purée using some of the stock. You may have to do this in batches.

Place the puréed kale into a large saucepan with the chicken cutlets and the amaranth.

Pour in the remaining stock and season with salt and pepper.

Bring to the boil, reduce the heat and simmer for about 45 minutes until the chicken is cooked and the soup has thickened.

When the soup is cooked, remove the chicken, shred finely and return to the soup.

To make the spice mix, heat the oil in a small frying pan and cook the garlic for about 30 seconds—be careful not to burn the garlic, as it will taste bitter. Stir in the coriander and cumin and cook for a few seconds until fragrant. Remove from the heat and pour into the soup immediately.

Leave to rest for about 10-15 minutes for all the flavours to combine, then serve garnished with some lemon zest and chilli flakes and a good sprinkle of lemon juice.

NOTE: THIS IS ONE OF MY FAVOURITE SOUPS AND THIS IS MY VERSION OF THE WELL-KNOWN EGYPTIAN SOUP MOLOKHIA, WHICH IS USUALLY MADE WITH THE LEAVES OF THE *CORCHORUS*, BUT HERE IS MADE WITH KALE.

COLCANNON WITH KALE

SERVES 4–6

2 lb 4 oz/1 kg potatoes
1 small bunch of kale
1-2 teaspoons butter
4 scallions/spring onions, sliced
2-3 tablespoons water
1½ tablespoons butter (extra)
¾ -1 cup milk
salt and freshly cracked black
    pepper

Scrub the potatoes and boil in salted water until tender.

In the meantime wash the kale thoroughly, remove and discard the tough stalks and finely chop the leaves.

Melt the butter in a large frying pan and sauté the scallions until soft, add the kale and continue cooking for about 7-10 minutes until the kale wilts and softens. At some point during the cooking time add the water to the kale to create some steam and soften the kale even more. Remove from the heat and set aside.

When the potatoes are cooked, drain, peel and finely mash. Return to the heat and stir in the extra butter and as much milk as is needed to make creamy and fluffy mashed potatoes.

Stir the kale into the potatoes until well combined and keep on a low heat until heated through.

Check and adjust seasoning and serve as a side dish with your favourite meat or vegetable dish.

NOTE: ALTHOUGH COLCANNON MAKES A GREAT SIDE DISH, I AM MORE THAN HAPPY TO EAT THIS ON ITS OWN. IF I AM AFTER A BOWL OF COMFORT, THIS IS IT.

IMPOSSIBLE KALE PIE

Preheat the oven to 350°F/180°C and lightly grease a
12 in/30 cm quiche dish.

Thoroughly wash the kale, remove and discard the thick
tough stalks. Finely chop the leaves and the more tender
upper stalks.

Heat the oil in a large frying pan and sauté the shallots
for 2-3 minutes until golden, add the kale and cook for
about 5 minutes, stirring regularly until the kale collapses.
Set aside to cool.

Whisk together the eggs, milk and cream. Slowly
incorporate the flour into the egg mixture, then stir in the
cheese. Season with salt and pepper to taste, keeping in
mind the saltiness of the cheese.

Stir the kale then pour the mixture into the prepared
dish.

Bake for about 30-40 minutes until the pie has set and
is golden on top.

Serve with a salad.

1 small bunch kale (about
   8 large stalks)
2 tablespoons extra virgin olive
   oil
6 scallions/spring onions, sliced
6 extra large eggs
10½ fl oz/300 ml low-fat milk
7 fl oz/200 ml low-fat cream
⅔ cup all-purpose/plain flour
¾ cup grated cheddar cheese
salt and freshly cracked pepper

NOTE: THIS PIE IS CALLED AN IMPOSSIBLE PIE BECAUSE IT IS
VIRTUALLY IMPOSSIBLE FOR IT TO GO WRONG—SOMETHING
HAPPENS DURING THE COOKING PROCESS WHERE THE PIE SORTS
ITSELF OUT AND SEPARATES INTO A BASE AND TOPPING ALL BY
ITSELF. FOR AN ALTERNATIVE, YOU CAN ADD SOME BACON, JUST
ADD AT THE SAME TIME AS WHEN YOU ARE SAUTÉING THE KALE.
IF YOU ARE GLUTEN OR WHEAT INTOLERANT, SUBSTITUTE THE
WHEATEN FLOUR WITH QUINOA FLOUR AND ADD 1 TEASPOON
BAKING POWDER TO THE QUINOA FLOUR.

FISH AND KALE STEW

SERVES 4–6

1 tablespoon extra virgin oil
1 chorizo sausage, diced
1 large onion, chopped
4 cloves garlic, finely chopped
1 teaspoon smoked paprika
2 x 14 oz/400 g cans diced
   tomatoes, undrained
1 cup chicken stock
1 large bunch kale
4 sprigs fresh thyme
1 teaspoon dried oregano
   leaves
1 bay leaf
salt and freshly cracked black
   pepper
1 x 14 oz/400 g can cannellini
   beans, rinsed and drained
4 fish fillets (see note below)
juice of 1 lemon, to taste
freshly chopped parsley, for
   garnish

Heat the oil in large, wide saucepan and cook the chorizo for 2-3 minutes, until it starts to change colour.

Add the onion and cook until soft, then stir in the garlic and paprika and cook for another 1-2 minutes.

Add the tomatoes and stock and give the pot a good stir. Wash the kale, remove and discard the thick tough stalks then finely chop the leaves and more tender upper stalks.

Add the kale to the saucepan and stir until it wilts.

Stir in the thyme, oregano, bay leaf and season with salt and pepper.

Bring to the boil, cover, reduce the heat and simmer on low-medium heat for 15 minutes.

Stir in the beans then place the fish on top of the stew, cover with some of the juices and simmer, covered for another 8-10 minutes or until the fish is cooked.

Squeeze some lemon juice over the stew and garnish with freshly chopped parsley.

Serve with crusty bread.

NOTE: IT IS BEST TO USE A MILD-TASTING, THICKISH FILLET FOR THIS DISH WITH A WEIGHT OF ABOUT 7 OZ/200 G EACH PIECE. SNAPPER, COD OR MULLOWAY WOULD BE IDEAL.

KALE WITH APPLE AND BACON

SERVES 4–6 AS A SIDE DISH

Thoroughly wash the kale, discard the tough stalks and finely shred the leaves and the upper, more tender, parts of the kale. Set side.

Dry roast the pine nuts in a large non-stick frying pan until golden, stirring regularly. Keep an eye on them as they can burn very quickly. Remove them from the pan and transfer onto another dish to stop the cooking process. Set aside.

Remove the rind and any excess fat from the bacon and slice into strips. Heat the oil in the frying pan add the bacon and cook until crisp. Remove from the pan, drain on kitchen paper and set aside.

Add the onion to the pan and sauté until soft. Add the kale to the pan and cook for 3-5 minutes until it collapses.

Pour in the apple juice, cover and cook on low heat for about 5-7 minutes until the kale softens.

Add the apples, season with salt and pepper, and cook for another 5 minutes or so until the apples are soft.

Stir in the pine nuts and bacon, heat through and serve.

1 bunch kale
2 oz/60 g pine nuts
1 tablespoon extra virgin olive oil
3 rashers bacon
1 large red onion, chopped
2 green apples, peeled and diced
½ cup apple juice
salt
freshly cracked black pepper

NOTE: THE APPLES AND APPLE JUICE ADD SWEETNESS TO THIS DISH, WHICH COMPLEMENTS THE BACON. FOR A VEGETARIAN OPTION, LEAVE OUT THE BACON. CASHEWS CAN BE SUBSTITUTED FOR THE PINE NUTS.

KALE, BEAN, ARTICHOKE AND OLIVE SALAD

SERVES 4–6

Thoroughly wash the kale, discard the thick stalks and finely shred the leaves.

Lightly steam the leaves or alternatively cook them in salted boiling water for 1-2 minutes only then drain and plunge into a bowl of iced water to stop the cooking process. Drain well.

Place the cooled kale into a large bowl and add the oil and vinegar, season with salt and pepper and gently rub the kale with this dressing. Toss well then leave to stand for about 5-10 minutes.

Halve the olives lengthways and cut the capsicums into strips. Add to the bowl with the kale, artichoke hearts, beans, capers, chillies and onion.

Toss well to combine all the ingredients together.

Taste and adjust the seasoning and dressing according to your taste.

1 bunch kale
4 tablespoons extra virgin olive oil
2 tablespoons red wine vinegar
salt and pepper
1 cup pitted black kalamata olives
5 oz/150 g char-grilled bell peppers/capsicums
9 oz/280 g jar artichoke hearts, cut into quarters
2 x 14 oz/400 g cans borlotti beans, rinsed and drained
2 tablespoons capers, drained
1-2 red chillies, seeded and chopped
1 small red onion, finely chopped

NOTE: YOU DON'T HAVE TO COOK THE KALE FOR THIS SALAD IF YOU DON'T WANT TO. THE KALE CAN BE USED RAW, JUST SHRED THE LEAVES VERY FINELY AND RUB WITH THE OIL, VINEGAR, SALT AND PEPPER AND LEAVE TO STAND FOR ABOUT 15-20 MINUTES BEFORE ADDING THE OTHER INGREDIENTS. SOME PEOPLE FIND THE RAW KALE TO BE A LITTLE BITTER ON THE TONGUE. THIS IS A LOVELY SALAD AND GREAT AS AN ACCOMPANIMENT WITH MEAT OR FISH. YOU CAN ROAST YOUR OWN PEPPERS OR USE READY-MADE IN A JAR.

KALE, CHICKPEA AND CARROT SALAD

SERVES 4–6

1 small bunch curly kale
2 x 14 oz/400 g cans
  chickpeas, drained
1 red bell pepper/capsicum
4-5 scallions/spring onions,
  sliced
2 medium carrots, peeled and
  coarsely grated
1 long red or green chilli,
  de-seeded and chopped
  (optional)

DRESSING
4 tablespoons extra virgin
  olive oil
juice of ½ -1 lemon
2 teaspoons Dijon mustard
salt
freshly ground black pepper

Thoroughly wash the kale and remove and discard the stalk, and finely shred the leaves.

Steam or cook the shredded kale in salted boiling water for 1-2 minutes only then drain and plunge into a bowl of iced water to stop the cooking process. Drain well.

Remove the seeds and membrane from the capsicum and cut into a small dice the size of the chickpeas.

Place the blanched kale and capsicum into a bowl with the scallions, carrot and the chilli if you choose.

Whisk together the olive oil and lemon juice with the mustard then season with salt and pepper.

Pour the dressing over the salad ingredients and toss well. If possible leave to stand for at about 1 hour before serving to allow all the flavours to combine.

NOTE: IF YOU PREFER, YOU CAN USE THE KALE RAW AND NOT COOK IT FIRST. IF YOU ARE GOING TO USE THE KALE RAW, RUB THE FINELY SHREDDED LEAVES IN THE DRESSING AND LEAVE TO STAND FOR 15-20 MINUTES IN THE DRESSING BEFORE ADDING THE OTHER INGREDIENTS.

KALE CHIPS

SERVES 4—6

Preheat the oven to 300°F/150°C and line 2-3 baking trays with non-stick baking paper.

Remove the leaves from the stem, wash and gently pat dry or better still use a salad spinner.

Place the kale leaves into a large bowl and toss with the oil and sea salt until well coated.

Spread onto the prepared trays without overcrowding them or they will not crisp up.

Place in the oven and bake for about 25 minutes. After 10 minutes turn them over. At this stage they will not be very crispy. Bake for another 10-15 minutes until they are thin and very crispy.

Instead of having plain salted kale chips, you could add some different flavourings to the oil and salt. Use the options listed or make your own.

1 bunch kale
extra virgin olive oil
sea salt
flavourings: chilli flakes, smoked paprika, cumin seeds or ground cumin, balsamic vinegar and sea salt, curry powder, chilli and lime zest, a sprinkling of soy sauce, flavoured salt, such as garlic or celery

NOTE: THESE ARE REALLY DELICIOUS AND VERY MOREISH WITH WHATEVER FLAVOURING YOU CHOOSE. IF YOU ARE LUCKY ENOUGH TO HAVE ANY LEFTOVER THESE KALE CHIPS CAN BE STORED IN AN AIRTIGHT CONTAINER AND WILL REMAIN FRESH AND CRISPY FOR ABOUT UP TO 2 DAYS.

KALE WITH BEANS AND TOASTED PINE NUTS

SERVES 2–4

3 oz/90 g pine nuts
3-4 tablespoons extra virgin
   olive oil
3 cloves garlic, sliced
2 cups fresh breadcrumbs
1 bunch kale
salt and freshly cracked pepper
1 x 14 oz/400 g can black or
   borlotti or cannellini beans
juice of 1 lemon, for serving

Dry roast the pine nuts in a large non-stick frying until golden. Keep an eye on them as they can burn very quickly. Remove from the pan and put into a dish and set aside.

Heat the oil in the frying pan until hot and sauté the garlic until it just starts to change colour.

Add the breadcrumbs and toss continually until they become totally coated in the oil and are toasted to a golden colour. Remove from the pan and set aside.

Thoroughly wash the kale and discard the thick stalks, shred the leaves and the more tender upper part of the stalk very finely.

Heat a little more oil in the pan, add the kale, season with salt and pepper and cook for about 5 minutes, stirring regularly until the kale collapses and softens.

At this stage you can add about 2 tablespoons of water to create a little steam and soften the kale more quickly.

Drain and rinse the beans then stir them into the kale with the breadcrumbs and pine nuts, and cook for another 5 minutes until the beans and breadcrumbs have heated through.

Serve with a sprinkle of lemon juice as a side dish or as a main meal.

NOTE: THIS IS A LOVELY DISH TO HAVE AS A MAIN MEAL OR AS A SIDE DISH. I OFTEN SERVE THIS AS A VEGETARIAN MEAL AS IS OR WITH COOKED RICE OR QUINOA.

KALE WITH CHICKEN, POTATOES AND OLIVES

SERVES 4

Combine the marinade ingredients and coat the chicken. Set aside for 15-20 minutes to marinate.

Boil the potatoes in salted water until tender but still firm. You can either leave them whole or cut them in half.

While the potatoes are cooking, thoroughly wash the kale, discard the thick tough stalks and cut the leaves and the upper more tender parts of the stalk into fine strips.

Heat oil in a large deep frying pan and cook the tomatoes until they start to blister, remove from the pan and set aside. Add the onion to the pan and cook until soft and golden.

Stir in the kale and toss until it is coated with the oil and continue cooking until the kale has wilted and is tender, about 5 minutes. Make sure to stir the pan regularly. Stir in the garlic and cook another minute or so until fragrant.

Drain the potatoes and add to the kale with the lemon juice and water and season with salt to taste and lots of pepper. Cover and cook on low heat for 10-15 minutes until the kale is tender.

Stir in the olives and tomatoes and drizzle with the extra olive oil.

Taste and adjust the seasoning.

Heat a medium frying pan over a high heat and grill or pan-fry the chicken until it is cooked and golden on both sides.

Serve the potato and tomato mixture with the chicken.

4 half chicken breast fillets
1 lb/500 g baby new potatoes
1 bunch of kale
1-2 tablespoons extra virgin olive oil
8 oz/250 g cherry or grape tomatoes
1 red onion, chopped
3-4 cloves of garlic, sliced
juice ½ -1 lemon
1 cup water
salt
freshly cracked black pepper
½ -1 cup pitted kalamata olives
1-2 tablespoons extra virgin olive oil (extra)

MARINADE

1 tablespoons extra virgin olive oil
½ teaspoon paprika
1 teaspoon dried oregano leaves
1-2 tablespoons lemon juice
salt and freshly ground black pepper

NOTE: THIS IS ONE OF MY FAVOURITE WAYS TO SERVE KALE. MY DAUGHTERS ARE VEGETARIANS AND I OFTEN MAKE THIS DISH WHEN WE ARE ALL TOGETHER, I JUST DON'T SERVE THEM ANY CHICKEN.

KALE LASAGNE

To make the white cheese sauce, melt butter in a saucepan, stir in flour and cook a few seconds until butter and flour are well incorporated and a roux has formed. Pour the milk in a little at a time and whisk until free of lumps. Continue stirring until sauce bubbles and thickens. Add the cheese and stir until it has melted and sauce is thick and velvety smooth. Season with salt and pepper to taste.

Heat oil in a large saucepan and sauté onion on high heat until golden. Add the minced beef and continue cooking on high heat until browned all over, breaking up any lumps as you go.

Stir in the garlic and cook until fragrant. Add the tomato paste and oregano and cook for 1-2 minutes.

Pour in the tomatoes and water and season with salt and pepper. Bring to the boil, reduce the heat and simmer on low heat, covered, for 10 minutes.

Wash the kale thoroughly, discard the tough stalks then finely chop the leaves and the upper more tender parts of the stalk.

Add the kale to the mince in batches and stir until it wilts. Stir in the nutmeg then taste and adjust the seasoning. Cover and simmer for about 10-15 minutes until the kale is cooked to your liking.

Preheat the oven to 350°F/180°C. Spread a thin layer of white sauce over the base of a deep lasagne dish. Line the dish with a layer of lasagne sheets and spread one-third of the kale sauce over the lasagne sheets. Repeat this process two more times, finishing with a layer of lasagne sheets. Cover with the cheese sauce and sprinkle some grated parmesan on top. Dust with some paprika and bake for 25-30 minutes until golden brown on top. Rest for a good 30 minutes if possible before cutting.

2 tablespoons extra virgin olive oil
1 large onion, finely chopped
1 lb/500 g ground/minced beef
3 cloves garlic, chopped
2 tablespoons tomato paste/purée
1 tablespoon dried oregano leaves
1 x 14 oz/400 g can diced tomatoes, undrained
2 cups water
salt and freshly cracked pepper
1 bunch kale
few grates of nutmeg
8 fresh lasagne sheets
grated parmesan
pinch paprika

WHITE CHEESE SAUCE
2 oz/60 g butter
4 tablespoons flour
3 cups milk
3/4 cup grated tasty cheese
salt and white pepper

NOTE: FOR A GLUTEN- /WHEAT-FREE OPTION, USE QUINOA FLOUR INSTEAD.

THIS IS A TWO-IN-ONE RECIPE. I SOMETIMES JUST MAKE THE KALE SAUCE WITH THE BEEF AND SERVE IT OVER COOKED QUINOA OR RICE.

KALE, PEA AND POTATO SOUP

SERVES 4—6

2 tablespoons extra virgin
  olive oil
2 leeks, washed well and
  finely sliced
3 cloves garlic, chopped
2 large potatoes, peeled
  and diced
2 carrots, diced
a good grate of nutmeg
few sprigs fresh thyme
1 large bunch kale, chopped
8 cups hot vegetable stock
salt and freshly cracked black
  pepper
2 cups frozen peas

Heat the oil in a large saucepan and sauté the leeks until soft. Add the garlic and cook until fragrant, about 30 seconds.

Add the potatoes and carrots, and cook for a few minutes until they start to soften. Stir in the nutmeg and thyme.

Thoroughly wash the kale, remove and discard the tough stalks and finely chop the leaves and some of the more tender upper stalks.

Add the kale to the pan and continue cooking until the kale starts to wilt.

Pour in the stock and season with salt and pepper. Bring the soup to the boil, reduce the heat, cover and simmer for about 15-20 minutes until the potatoes are cooked and kale tender.

Add the peas straight from the freezer, bring the soup back to the boil, reduce the heat, cover and simmer for about 5-7 minutes until the peas are tender.

Check and adjust the seasoning and serve with crusty bread.

NOTE: THIS IS A VERY HEALTHY VEGETABLE SOUP AND A MEAL ON ITS OWN. IF YOU WANTED TO ADD MORE BULK YOU COULD STIR IN SOME RINSED QUINOA WHEN YOU ADD THE STOCK. THE QUINOA WILL ABSORB SOME LIQUID SO YOU WILL NEED TO ADD A LITTLE MORE STOCK.

KALE, PUMPKIN AND CHICKPEA SOUP

Thoroughly wash the kale, remove and discard the thick tough stalks and finely chop the leaves and some of the more tender stalks and set aside.

Thoroughly wash the leek and slice finely, heat the oil in a large saucepan and sauté the leek until soft then add the garlic and cook for about 30 seconds.

Stir in the cumin, coriander, turmeric, cinnamon, ginger, fennel seeds and chilli, and cook for just a few seconds until fragrant.

Add the kale to the pot with the tomatoes and the stock. Season with salt and pepper, bring to the boil, reduce the heat and simmer for 20 minutes.

Remove the cinnamon stick and purée the soup, return to the boil and add the pumpkin, chickpeas and the extra can of tomatoes.

Bring back to the boil, reduce the heat, cover and simmer on low heat for 15-20 minutes until the pumpkin is cooked.

Leave to stand for about 15 minutes before serving with a good squeeze of lemon or lime juice, a sprinkling of chopped fresh cilantro and lots of crusty bread.

1 large bunch kale
2 tablespoons extra virgin olive oil or pure coconut oil
1 large leek
3 cloves garlic
2 teaspoons ground cumin
1 teaspoon ground coriander
1 teaspoon ground turmeric
1 cinnamon stick
1 teaspoon ground ginger
1 teaspoon fennel seeds
1/4 - 1/2 teaspoon chilli powder
1 x 14 oz/400 g can diced tomatoes, undrained
8 cups chicken or vegetable stock
salt and pepper
24 oz/750 g butternut squash/ pumpkin, cubed
1 x 14 oz/400 g can chickpeas, drained
1 x 14 oz/400 g can diced tomatoes, undrained (extra)
lemon or lime juice, for serving
fresh cilantro/coriander, for serving (optional)

NOTE: THIS IS ONE OF MY FAVOURITE SOUPS—VERY HEARTY, FILLING, WITH LOTS OF SPICES. REALLY LOVELY ON A WINTER'S DAY.

KALE, CHORIZO AND BEAN SOUP

SERVES 4

2 tablespoons extra virgin olive
  oil
2-3 chorizo sausages, sliced
1 large onion, chopped
2 cloves garlic, chopped
1 bunch kale
6 cups chicken or beef stock
2 x 14 oz/400 g cans cannellini
  beans, drained
salt and pepper, to taste

Heat the oil in a large saucepan and sauté the chorizo sausages until golden. Remove from the pan with a slotted spoon and set aside.

Add the onion to the saucepan and sauté until soft. Stir in garlic and cook for about 1 minute until fragrant.

Thoroughly wash the kale, remove and discard the thick tough stalks and finely shred the leaves and some of the more tender stalks. Add to the saucepan, stir and cook for about 3-5 minutes until the kale wilts.

Pour in the stock and bring to the boil, reduce the heat, cover and simmer for 10-15 minutes.

Add the beans and chorizo sausage, bring back to the boil, reduce the heat and simmer, covered, for 5-10 minutes until the kale is tender.

Season with salt and pepper to taste and serve with a good squeeze of lemon juice and some crusty bread.

NOTE: THIS IS A REALLY EASY AND QUICK TO PREPARE SOUP. YOU CAN SUBSTITUTE BACON FOR THE CHORIZO OR, FOR A VEGETARIAN OPTION, LEAVE OUT THE CHORIZO ALTOGETHER.

KALE AND EGGS FOR BREAKFAST

SERVES 2

Heat oil and butter in a large frying pan and sauté the onion until soft and golden.

Add the tomatoes and cook for 2-3 minutes until they start to break down.

Thoroughly wash the kale and remove the thick tough stalks, finely chop the leaves and add the pan.

Cook until the kale collapses then stir in the Worcestershire sauce and as much of the water needed to create some moisture for the kale to soften and cook.

Cook for about 5 minutes until the kale is tender.

Make 4 spaces in the pan among the vegetables and gently crack an egg into each one.

Cook on gentle heat until the eggs are set to your liking. Season with salt and pepper and serve on toast.

2 tablespoons extra virgin olive oil
1 small onion, finely chopped
2 large tomatoes, skinned and cut into chunks
6 large kale leaves
2-3 teaspoons Worcestershire sauce
1/4 - 1/2 cup water
4 eggs
salt and freshly cracked pepper

NOTE: THIS DISH IS IDEAL NOT ONLY FOR BREAKFAST BUT ALSO FOR BRUNCH, LUNCH OR A LIGHT SUPPER. TO SKIN THE TOMATOES, CUT A LITTLE CROSS AT THE BOTTOM OF EACH ONE AND PLACE IN BOILING WATER FOR ABOUT ONE MINUTE. REMOVE FROM THE WATER WITH A FORK AS THEY WILL BE QUITE HOT, AND REMOVE THE SKIN, WHICH SHOULD PEEL OFF QUITE EASILY.

MUSHROOMS FILLED WITH KALE AND BACON

SERVES 4–6

1 cup quinoa, rinsed and drained

2 cups water

6 extra large mushrooms

1 tablespoon extra virgin olive oil

3 rashers bacon, rind removed and chopped

1 medium red onion, finely chopped

1 tablespoon tomato paste/purée

2 cloves garlic, finely chopped

1 tablespoon fresh thyme leaves

6-8 large stalks of kale

1 cup chicken stock or water

salt and freshly cracked black pepper

3 oz/90 g pine nuts

3 large cherry tomatoes

Place quinoa into a small saucepan with the water and bring to the boil. Reduce the heat, cover and simmer for 10 minutes until all the water is absorbed and the quinoa is cooked. Leave to stand, covered, while you prepare the other ingredients.

Gently wipe over the mushrooms and remove the stalks.

Preheat the oven to 350°F/180°C and line a baking tray with non-stick paper.

Heat the oil in a non-stick frying pan and sauté the bacon and onion until lightly browned. Stir in the tomato paste, garlic and thyme, and cook for about 1 minute.

Thoroughly wash the kale, remove and discard the tough stalks and finely chop the leaves and some of the more tender stalks. Add the kale to the pan and cook until it starts to wilt.

Pour in the stock or water, season with a little salt and a good grind of pepper and cook for about 5 minutes, covered, until the kale is tender.

Do not allow the kale to go dry; if it looks like it is, add a little more water to the pan. Remove the pan from the heat and stir in the quinoa and the pine nuts.

Divide the mixture into 6 and fill the underside of each mushroom with the filling, piling it up high and place into the baking dish.

Slice the tomatoes in half and place a half tomato on top of each mushroom, drizzle with olive oil and bake for about 20 minutes.

NOTE: YOU CAN OMIT THE BACON FOR A VEGETARIAN OPTION. IF THE MUSHROOM STALKS ARE NOT TOO WOODY, YOU CAN CHOP THEM INTO SMALL PIECES AND ADD TO THE KALE FILLING. YOU CAN SERVE ONE OR TWO MUSHROOMS PER PERSON DEPENDING ON HOW BIG THEY ARE.

QUINOA

Quinoa, pronounced keen-wah, is an ancient seed native to the Andes Mountains in South America. It has been around for over 5,000 years and is known to have been a staple food of the ancient civilisation of the Incas, having sustained them for centuries.

It was used to supplement their diet of potatoes and corn. It was commonly referred to as the 'mother grain' or 'gold of the Incas' and was considered sacred. It is still considered a very important food in South American kitchens and now the whole world is catching on to this little supergrain to make it a superfood. I have always referred to quinoa as the supergrain of the century.

Although most commonly referred to as a grain, quinoa is actually a seed. It is the seed of a leafy plant called *Chenopodium quinoa* of the *Chenopodium/goosefoot* plant family and is distantly related to the spinach plant.

Of all the supergrains, quinoa is my absolute favourite. This would explain why I have written three cookbooks all on quinoa and all featuring quinoa as the main ingredient in every single dish.

In a nutshell, quinoa is a complete source of protein and has all the essential amino acids, trace elements and vitamins needed to survive.

It is considered to be almost a complete food, being very high in protein, full of vitamins, totally gluten-, wheat- and cholesterol-free, usually organic and of absolute great benefit to everyone's diet. It is also very easy to prepare and tastes absolutely delicious.

It has a very high level of protein, more than most other grains, and this unusually large amount of protein is actually a complete protein containing all nine essential amino acids.

The amino acid composition is extremely well balanced and has a particularly high content of the amino acid lysine, which is essential in our diet for tissue repair and growth. Quinoa is a must for vegans and vegetarians who may be concerned about the level of protein in their daily diet.

It is also a very good source of manganese, magnesium, potassium, phosphorous, copper, zinc and vitamins E, B6, riboflavin, niacin and thiamine. It has more calcium than cow's milk, is an excellent antioxidant, is rich in dietary fibre and has more iron than any other grain. It also has the highest content of unsaturated fats and a lower ratio of carbohydrates than any other grain, plus a low glycaemic index. The health benefits to be gained from using this grain are truly enormous.

Quinoa has a huge range of uses and lends itself to so many dishes. When cooked it has a very delicate texture and is lovely in soups and sweets, and makes wonderful salads, pasta and breads.

Varieties of quinoa

The grain itself is tiny and round with a fine band around it ending in what looks like a minute 'tail'. As it cooks the 'tail' spirals out and almost detaches itself. It becomes very distinct from the rest of the grain in the shape of an outer white ring that is clearly visible. When cooked the grain becomes very soft in the centre while the 'tail' retains a bit of crunch giving it a texture all of its own.

When the grain is cooked it has a very delicate texture and it expands to almost four times its original volume.

There are three varieties: black, white and red. The white variety is most commonly available, but the red and black varieties hold their shape better once cooked. Quinoa also comes in flake or flour form.

The distinct nutty taste is more pronounced in the flour, giving it an earthy aroma. The flour can also be slightly bitter, which I find can be counterbalanced by the other sweeter or aromatic ingredients used in a recipe. The flakes are great used as a substitute for normal breadcrumbs, especially for stuffings and coatings.

Which coloured grain you wish to use in your cooking is totally up to you. I have specified a colour in only a few recipes purely for visual appeal.

Preparation

Quinoa has a bitter outer-coating called saponin. This soapy like substance must be removed before cooking. Although most grain comes pre-washed and ready to cook, it is still a good idea to rinse it thoroughly before use to remove any residue of saponin.

Place the quinoa in a fine sieve and rinse under cold running water. After thoroughly wetting the quinoa, rub it lightly between your fingertips, drain well and it is ready to cook. Make sure that you do use a very fine sieve as the grains are so tiny they will otherwise go straight through a standard colander or strainer.

Quinoa cooks very quickly simmered in water, stock, juice or milk. Cook one part quinoa to two parts liquid for 10 minutes in the saucepan. However, you may need to cook the quinoa a little longer if the liquid is denser than water, such as a sauce, stock or milk. Also the red and black varieties take a little longer to cook and tend to retain a little bit more of a crunch. The length of the cooking time can also vary depending on the brand and age of the grain. Resting the cooked quinoa, covered, for 10–15 minutes after cooking will ensure it is softer and fluffier. Use a fork to fluff up the quinoa after it has been cooked.

BREAKFAST BARS

MAKES ABOUT 20

3/4 cup quinoa flour
1 teaspoon gluten-free baking
   powder
1 cup quinoa flakes
1 teaspoon ground cinnamon
3/4 cup brown sugar
4 oz/125 g dried cranberries
4 oz/125 g cup dried apricots,
   chopped
3 oz/90 g golden raisins/
   sultanas
4 oz/125 g sunflower seeds
2 oz/60 g slivered almonds,
   chopped
1 3/4 oz/50 g butter
1/3 cup honey
1 teaspoon vanilla bean paste
2 extra large eggs, lightly
   beaten

Preheat the oven to 350°F/180°C and lightly grease a 12 x 7½ in/29 x 19 cm slice tin, then line with baking paper. Greasing the tin first helps the paper stay in place.

Sift flour and baking powder into a large bowl then stir in the quinoa flakes, cinnamon and sugar, and mix well, making sure you break up any lumps in the sugar.

Add the cranberries, apricots, raisins, sunflower seeds and almonds and mix well to combine.

Place the butter and honey into a small saucepan and stir over low heat until the butter has melted and then stir in the vanilla.

Pour the melted butter and the eggs over the flour and fruit mixture and mix really well, pressing the mixture together so it is well combined and not dry.

Using the back of a spoon, press the mixture firmly into the prepared tin and bake for about 20-25 minutes, until golden.

Remove from the oven and leave to cool in the tin for about 15 minutes and then cut into desired sized bars. Leave to cool in the tin for a little longer then carefully remove the slice with the paper and place on a cooling rack to cool completely.

NOTE: THESE BARS ARE GREAT FOR BREAKFAST ON THE RUN OR FOR A QUICK BUT SATISFYING AND NOURISHING SNACK. PACK THEM INTO SCHOOL AND WORK LUNCH BOXES, TAKE THEM TO PICNICS OR ENJOY THEM AS AN AFTER-SPORT SNACK.

BLUEBERRY FRIANDS

Preheat the oven to 325°F/170°C. Grease a 9-cup friand tin with butter.

Place the almond meal, icing sugar and quinoa flour into a bowl. Using a whisk, mix well, breaking up any lumps of mixture that may have formed.

Lightly mix in the butter and vanilla extract.

Beat the egg whites until foamy and soft peaks form, gently fold into the mixture.

Spoon the mixture evenly into the prepared tin.

Place 6-8 blueberries around the centre of each friand and lightly press them down into the mixture.

Bake for about 25 minutes until lightly browned and cooked when tested with a metal skewer.

4 oz/125 g almond meal
1 cup pure confectioner's/icing
  sugar, sifted
⅓ cup quinoa flour
4 oz/125 g unsalted butter,
  melted and cooled
½ teaspoon vanilla extract
4 large eggwhites
8 oz/250 g fresh blueberries

NOTE: YOU CAN SUBSTITUTE THE BLUEBERRIES WITH RASPBERRIES OR BLACKBERRIES IF YOU PREFER. I USUALLY LIKE TO MAKE A DOUBLE QUANTITY OF THESE AS THEY JUST DON'T LAST.

CRUNCHY BREAKFAST MIX

MAKES 8 CUPS

Place the quinoa into a small saucepan with the water. Bring to the boil, reduce the heat and simmer for 10 minutes until all the water is absorbed. Remove from the heat, uncover and cool completely.

Preheat the oven to 325°F/ 160°C and line 2 large baking trays with non-stick baking paper.

In a large bowl mix together the quinoa flakes, cooled quinoa grain, almonds, pepitas, sunflower and sesame seeds, cinnamon and nutmeg.

Add the vanilla, maple syrup, brown sugar, honey and oil and mix really well as you want all the ingredients to be completely coated.

Spread the mixture out evenly over the 2 trays in a single layer and bake for about 30-40 minutes until crisp and crunchy and a rich golden colour. Stir once or twice through the baking time, making sure you keep the mix evenly distributed in the tray.

Remove from the oven and cool, then stir in the raisins and cranberries and store in an airtight container when completely cold.

Serve with milk or yoghurt or sprinkle over porridge.

¾ cup red quinoa, rinsed and drained

1½ cups water

1½ cups quinoa flakes

4 oz/125 g whole blanched almonds

2½ oz/75 g pepitas/pumpkin seeds

2½ oz/75 g sunflower seeds

2 oz/60 g sesame seeds

2 teaspoons ground cinnamon

½ teaspoon ground nutmeg

1 tablespoon vanilla paste or extract

⅓ cup maple syrup

⅓ cup light brown sugar, tightly packed

⅓ cup honey

2 tablespoons vegetable or extra light olive oil

5 oz/150 g golden raisins/ sultanas

4 oz/125 g dried cranberries

NOTE: THIS IS ONE OF THOSE MIXES THAT IS GOOD TO HAVE ON HAND AS IT IS NOT ONLY GREAT FOR BREAKFAST. YOU CAN ALSO GRAB A HANDFUL OF THIS AT ANY TIME. GOOD IN SCHOOL OR WORK LUNCHES. IF YOU DON'T HAVE MAPLE SYRUP YOU CAN USE GOLDEN SYRUP INSTEAD. KEEP AN EYE ON IT WHILE IT IS IN THE OVEN AS IT CAN BURN EASILY. I HAVE USED THE RED QUINOA IN THIS RECIPE PURELY FOR THE ADDED CRUNCH THAT YOU GET FROM THE DARKER GRAIN.

MOROCCAN-STYLE QUINOA AND SWEET POTATO

SERVES 6–8

Preheat the oven to 400°F/200°C and line a large baking tray with non-stick baking paper.

Drizzle the sweet potato with a little oil and season with salt and pepper, place on the tray and roast for about 20-30 minutes until tender and a little charred.

In the meantime, place quinoa into a medium-sized saucepan with the water, bring to the boil, reduce the heat, cover and simmer for 12-15 minutes until all the water is absorbed and the quinoa is cooked.

Remove from the heat and leave to stand, covered, while you prepare the remaining ingredients.

Heat the oil in a large frying pan and sauté the onion until soft, add the garlic, chilli, ginger and turmeric and cook for about 2 minutes until all the flavours combine.

Stir in the ground cumin and coriander, cumin seeds, coriander and fennel seeds, and cook until fragrant.

Add the chickpeas and a little water to create some steam so the pan is not completely dry, and cook for 4-5 minutes, then add the quinoa and toss well to combine everything together and the quinoa has heated through.

Gently toss in the pumpkin, fresh coriander, mint and the lime/lemon juice.

Serve with a dollop of Greek yoghurt.

2 lb 4 oz/1 kg kumera/orange sweet potato, peeled and diced

2 tablespoons extra virgin olive oil or coconut oil

1½ cups tri-coloured quinoa, rinsed and drained

3 cups water

1 large red onion, chopped

3 cloves garlic, finely chopped

1-2 long red chillies, de-seeded and chopped

1 tablespoon freshly grated ginger

1 tablespoon grated fresh turmeric

1 teaspoon ground cumin

1 teaspoon ground coriander

1 teaspoon cumin seeds

1 teaspoon fennel seeds

2 x 14 oz/400 g cans chickpeas/garbanzo beans, drained

½ cup chopped fresh cilantro/coriander

½ cup chopped fresh mint

juice 1-2 limes or lemons

Greek yoghurt, for serving

NOTE: THIS IS A REALLY GOOD DISH TO PREPARE WHEN YOU ARE FEEDING A CROWD OF VEGETARIANS OR AS A VEGETABLE SIDE DISH TO ACCOMPANY A MEAT MAIN.

MUSTARD CRUSTED SALMON WITH DILL AND LEMON

SERVES 4

Preheat the oven to 350°F/180°C.

Trim the salmon fillets to an even shape and place skin side down on a roasting tray that has been lined with non-stick baking paper.

Place mustard in a bowl with dill, parsley, garlic, lemon zest, juice, scallion and olive oil, and mix thoroughly to combine.

Mix in the quinoa flakes, salt and pepper. Use your hand to mix and squeeze mixture together so it holds.

Divide mixture into 4 and spread evenly on top of each fillet.

Drizzle with extra olive oil and bake for 15-20 minutes until topping is golden and salmon is cooked.

Serve with a squeeze of lemon juice and sprigs of dill.

4 salmon fillets, approx. 7 oz/200 g each
2 tablespoons Dijon mustard
3 tablespoons chopped fresh dill
2 tablespoons chopped fresh flat-leaf parsley
1 large clove garlic, grated
zest of 1 lemon
2-3 tablespoons lemon juice
1 scallion/shallot, finely sliced, including the greens
1 tablespoon olive oil, plus extra for drizzling
1 cup quinoa flakes
salt and freshly cracked pepper
juice of 1 lemon to serve
dill sprigs, to serve

NOTE: A DELICIOUS AND DIFFERENT WAY TO SERVE SALMON. LOVELY FOR A LUNCHEON SERVED WITH A BIG SALAD.

QUINOA CRACKERS WITH HUMMUS

MAKES ABOUT 40 CRACKERS

1 cup quinoa flour
1 teaspoon gluten-free baking
   powder
1 cup quinoa flakes
1 teaspoon sea salt
1 teaspoon cumin seeds
¼ – ½ teaspoon sweet paprika
3 teaspoons extra virgin
   olive oil
⅔ cup warm water

HUMMUS
1 x 14 oz/400 g can chickpeas,
   drained and rinsed
⅓ cup water (approx.)
¼ cup tahini paste
2 cloves garlic, finely grated
¼ cup lemon juice
1 tablespoon extra virgin
   olive oil
salt and freshly ground black
   pepper, to taste
extra virgin olive oil (for
   garnish)
ground sweet paprika (for
   garnish)

Preheat the oven to 400°F/ 200°C and line 2 baking trays with non-stick baking paper.

Sift flour and baking powder into a bowl and stir in the quinoa flakes, salt, cumin and paprika.

Mix in the olive oil and enough warm water to bind the dough together. You will more than likely use all the amount indicated.

Push the dough together into a ball and then use a floured rolling pin to roll out thinly onto a sheet of baking paper and cut into desired shapes.

Place the shapes onto the prepared trays and bake until golden, about 10-12 minutes, depending on the thickness of the crackers. Keep an eye on them as they can burn fairly quickly, ideally you want them not to be too soft when they come out of the oven. Cool completely in tray.

To make the hummus: place all ingredients into a food processor or blender and process until smooth. Taste and adjust the seasoning and amount of lemon juice.

Refrigerate for at least 2-3 hours before serving. Serve spread onto a shallow bowl garnished with a drizzle of oil and a sprinkle of paprika.

NOTE: RAW ORGANIC COCONUT OIL CAN BE SUBSTITUTED FOR THE EXTRA VIRGIN OLIVE OIL IN THE CRACKERS.

ALMOND AND COCONUT SALAD

SERVES 4–6

1 cup quinoa, rinsed and
   drained
2 cups water
5 oz/150 g whole almonds,
   skin on
1 cup moist coconut flakes
2 medium carrots, julienned or
   coarsely grated
4-6 scallions/spring onions,
   sliced
1-2 long red chillies, de-seeded
   and chopped
½ cup fresh chopped cilantro/
   coriander
2-3 tablespoons organic raw
   coconut oil or extra virgin
   olive oil
juice of 1-2 limes
salt and freshly cracked pepper

Place quinoa into a saucepan with the water. Bring to the boil, reduce the heat, cover and simmer on low heat for 10 minutes until all the water is absorbed. Remove from the heat, leave to stand for 10 minutes covered then cool completely.

Place the cooled quinoa into a large bowl with the almonds and the coconut flakes.

Julienne or coarsely grate the carrots and add to the quinoa with the scallions.

De-seed or leave the seeds in the chillies, and chop, add to the bowl with the coriander.

Mix together the coconut oil and as much lime juice as you like, pour into the salad and mix well.

Season with salt and pepper to taste.

NOTE: YOU CAN FIND MOIST COCONUT FLAKES AT MOST SUPERMARKETS AND ARE USUALLY IN THE DRIED FRUIT SECTION. IF YOU CAN'T FIND THEM YOU CAN USE SHREDDED COCONUT. THIS SALAD WORKS WELL WITH EITHER COCONUT OIL OR EXTRA VIRGIN OLIVE OIL.

HERB-CRUMBED CHICKEN TENDERLOINS

SERVES 6

Trim any fat and any bits of tendons from the tenderloins.

Combine the quinoa flakes with the thyme, chives, salt and pepper.

Dust the tenderloins with flour, dip them in the beaten egg then coat with the flake mixture, pressing down to make sure the tenderloins are well covered.

Heat the oil until hot and gently shallow fry on a medium heat, about 3 minutes on each side, until they are cooked and golden brown. Remove from the pan with a slotted spoon and place on kitchen paper to drain any excess oil.

2 lb 4 oz/1 kg chicken breast
   tenderloins
1½ cups quinoa flakes
1 tablespoon chopped fresh
   thyme
1 tablespoon chopped fresh
   chives
salt and freshly cracked black
   pepper
3/4 cup quinoa flour
2-3 eggs, lightly beaten
oil, for shallow frying

NOTE: IF YOU PREFER YOU CAN LEAVE OUT THE HERBS OR SUBSTITUTE THEM WITH ANY OTHER FAVOURITES. EITHER WAY THESE ARE ALWAYS A GREAT HIT AND KIDS LOVE THEM. MY FAMILY ENJOY THESE SERVED WITH A THAI SWEET CHILLI SAUCE.

QUINOA WITH CURRIED LENTILS

SERVES 4

Place quinoa into a medium saucepan with the water. Bring to the boil, reduce the heat, cover and simmer for 12-15 minutes until all the water is absorbed. Leave to stand covered for 5-10 minutes until needed.

Heat oil in a large frying pan add the garlic and chillies and cook for about 30 seconds until fragrant.

Stir the curry powder into the garlic and chillies, and cook for another minute or so.

Add the undrained lentils, season with salt and pepper to taste, and cook for 2-3 minutes for all the flavours to combine.

Stir in the quinoa, mix well continue cooking until the quinoa has heated through.

Stir in the cilantro and lemon juice and serve.

1½ cups tri-coloured quinoa, rinsed and drained

3 cups water

2 tablespoons extra virgin olive oil

2-3 cloves garlic, finely chopped

1-2 long red chillies, de-seeded and chopped

2 teaspoons curry powder

2 x 14 oz/400 g cans lentils, undrained

salt and freshly ground black pepper

good handful chopped fresh cilantro/coriander

juice ½ -1 lemon

NOTE: THIS IS A REALLY GOOD DISH TO MAKE ON A WORK NIGHT OR FOR LUNCH. IT IS VERY QUICK TO PREPARE, ESPECIALLY IF YOU HAVE THE QUINOA READY COOKED IN THE REFRIGERATOR. THIS DISH CAN BE EATEN HOT OR COLD AND IS GREAT TO TAKE TO WORK FOR LUNCH.

QUINOA WITH KALE, TOMATOES AND BLACK BEANS

SERVES 4

1 cup quinoa, rinsed and
  drained
2 cups water
2 tablespoons extra virgin olive
  oil
1 large onion, chopped
3 cloves garlic, chopped
1½ tablespoons ground cumin
1 tablespoon ground coriander
½ -1 teaspoon chilli flakes or to
  taste
2 x 14 oz/400 g cans cherry
  tomatoes, undrained
1 bunch kale, stalks removed
  and chopped
2 x 14 oz/400 g cans black
  beans, drained
salt, to taste
Greek yoghurt, for serving
juice of 1 lemon

Place the quinoa in a small saucepan with the water, bring to the boil, then reduce the heat, cover and simmer for 10 minutes until all the water is absorbed. Leave to stand covered until needed.

Heat oil in a large saucepan and sauté onion until it is lightly browned.

Stir in the garlic and cook for about 30 seconds until fragrant, take the pan off the heat and stir in the cumin, coriander and chilli.

Return the pan to the heat and cook spices on medium heat for about 1 minute stirring constantly so that the spices don't burn.

Add the tomatoes, kale and black beans, season with salt then bring to the boil, reduce the heat, cover and simmer for about 10-15 minutes until the kale is tender. Add a little water if the kale and lentils seem dry.

Stir in the quinoa, mix well and continue cooking for another 5 minutes until heated through. Serve with a dollop of Greek yoghurt and a squeeze of lemon juice.

NOTE: THIS IS ONE OF THOSE QUICK SATISFYING AND NOURISHING MEALS YOU CAN JUST THROW TOGETHER WHEN YOU GET HOME FROM WORK. IT IS ESPECIALLY QUICK TO PREPARE IF YOU ALREADY HAVE SOME COOKED QUINOA IN YOUR FRIDGE WHICH IS ALWAYS A GOOD IDEA TO HAVE.

EDAMAME BEAN SALAD

SERVES 6—8

½ cup black quinoa, rinsed
    and drained
½ cup red quinoa, rinsed and
    drained
2 cups water
1 red bell pepper/capsicum
1 yellow bell pepper/capsicum
2 cups shelled edamame
    beans
1 red onion, finely chopped
3-4 tablespoons finely
    chopped flat leaf parsley

DRESSING
3 tablespoons extra virgin
    olive oil
3 tablespoons rice vinegar or
    red wine vinegar
1 tablespoon honey
salt and freshly cracked pepper

Place the quinoa into a small saucepan with the water. Bring to the boil. Reduce the heat, cover and simmer for 12-15 minutes until all the water is absorbed.

Remove from the heat and stand, covered, for 10 minutes then cool completely.

Remove the seeds and membrane from the peppers and dice into small pieces. Combine the peppers with the quinoa, edamame beans, onion and parsley.

Mix the dressing ingredients together and pour over the salad. Mix well and, if possible, leave to stand for 30 minutes before serving.

NOTE: AS AN ALTERNATIVE YOU CAN ADD COOKED CHICKEN TO THIS SALAD. EDAMAME BEANS ARE AVAILABLE FROZEN, ALREADY BLANCHED AND IN THEIR SHELLS. IF BUYING THEM FROZEN, DEFROST THEM BEFORE REMOVING THE SHELLS.

SPICED MOROCCAN LAMB CUTLETS

SERVES 4

12 lamb cutlets
1 cup quinoa flakes
1 teaspoon ground cumin
1 teaspoon cumin seeds
½ teaspoon ground coriander
1 teaspoon ground paprika
¼ teaspoon ground cinnamon
½ -1 teaspoon chilli flakes
salt
2 tablespoons quinoa crispies
   (optional)
zest of 1 lemon
3 cloves garlic, finely grated
3 tablespoons chopped flat-leaf
   parsley
½ cup quinoa flour
2 eggs, lightly beaten
olive oil for cooking
lemon wedges, for serving

Trim the cutlets and gently pound to thin out just a little and set aside.

Mix together the flakes, ground cumin and seeds, ground coriander, paprika, cinnamon, chilli, salt and quinoa crispies.

Rub in the lemon zest, garlic and parsley, and mix well.

Dust the lamb cutlets with the quinoa flour then dip into and coat well with the egg.

Press firmly into the flake mixture making sure the cutlets are evenly coated.

Heat some oil in a large pan and shallow-fry the cutlets until the coating is crisp and golden about 3 minutes each side.

Serve with lemon juice squeezed over the top.

NOTE: I HAVE ALLOWED THREE CUTLETS PER PERSON, BUT TO BE PERFECTLY HONEST YOU MAY WANT TO PREPARE A FEW EXTRA. I ALWAYS FIND THAT WHEN I SERVE THESE THEY TEND TO JUST DISAPPEAR. QUINOA CRISPIES ARE QUINOA GRAIN THAT HAS BEEN TOASTED. THEY ARE AVAILABLE AT MOST HEALTH FOOD STORE.

SPANISH CHICKEN

Rub the chicken with the paprika until well coated. Heat the oil and melt butter in a large deep frying pan and brown the chicken all over on medium-high heat, until almost half cooked and a deep golden colour. Remove from the pan and keep warm by covering with foil.

Add the onion to the pan and cook until soft, stir in the garlic and cook until fragrant.

Lightly crush the saffron and add to the pan with the lemon zest, and season with salt and pepper.

Add the quinoa and stock, stirring everything together well, then return the chicken pieces to the pan and nestle in with the quinoa.

Bring to the boil, reduce the heat, cover and simmer for about 10 minutes. Scatter the olives over the chicken, cover and simmer for another 5-8 minutes until all the liquid is absorbed. Take off the heat and leave to stand for 5-10 minutes.

Sprinkle with the parsley and drizzle over some lemon juice before serving.

2 lb 4 oz/1 kg chicken thigh fillets, skinless
½ -1 teaspoons smoked paprika
1 tablespoon extra virgin olive oil
1 tablespoon ghee butter
1 large onion, chopped
3 cloves garlic, finely chopped
½ teaspoons saffron strands
zest of 1 lemon
salt and pepper, to taste
1½ cups quinoa, rinsed and drained
3 cups hot chicken stock
1 cup green stuffed olives
½ cup chopped flat-leaf parsley
juice of 1 lemon

NOTE: THIS IS ONE OF THOSE QUICK AND REALLY EASY TO PREPARE MEALS THAT ARE PERFECT FOR DINNER AFTER WORK OR WHEN UNEXPECTED GUESTS DROP BY.

QUINOA LAKSA

Heat the oil in a large saucepan and sauté the onion until soft, stir in the garlic and cook for a few seconds until fragrant.

Stir in the laksa paste then pour in the coconut milk with the stock and bring to the boil.

Add the quinoa, reduce the heat, cover and simmer for about 20 minutes.

Wash the bok choy and cut into quarters lengthways, leave the lower bulb part in quarters and shred the leaves.

Add to the soup with the snow peas and mushrooms, bring back to the boil, reduce the heat and simmer, covered, for another 8-10 minutes, until the quinoa is cooked and the vegetables are tender.

Take off the heat and leave to stand, covered, for 5-10 minutes before serving.

Serve garnished with freshly squeezed lime juice, bean sprouts, sliced chillies and cilantro leaves.

1 tablespoon organic raw coconut oil

1 large red onion, chopped

2 cloves garlic, finely chopped

4 tablespoons laksa paste

2 x 14 fl oz/400 ml cans low-fat coconut milk

4 cups vegetable stock

⅔ cup red quinoa, rinsed and drained

3 bunches baby bok choy,

5 oz/150 g snow peas, finely shredded

5 oz/150 g fresh shiitake mushrooms, sliced

lime juice

bean sprouts, for garnish

sliced red and green chillies, for garnish

fresh cilantro/coriander leaves for garnish

NOTE: YOU CAN VARY THE VEGETABLES USED TO SUIT YOUR TASTE. YOU MAY HAVE TO INCREASE OR DECREASE THE AMOUNT OF LAKSA PASTE YOU USE DEPENDING ON HOW MILD OR SPICY IT IS. IF YOU ARE UNABLE TO FIND LAKSA PASTE YOU CAN USE YOUR FAVOURITE CURRY PASTE INSTEAD.
IF YOU WISH, YOU CAN ALSO ADD GREEN PEELED SHRIMP/PRAWNS OR FINELY SLICED CHICKEN TO THE SOUP IN THE LAST 10 MINUTES OF COOKING TIME.

QUINOA SALAD WITH KALE, POMEGRANATE AND CURRANTS

SERVES 6–8

1 cup quinoa, rinsed and drained

2 cups water

1 small bunch of kale (about 4-6 large stalks)

1 small red onion or half a medium onion, finely chopped

1 cup currants

3 oz/90 g pine nuts

1 large pomegranate

3 oz/90 g feta cheese, crumbled (optional)

DRESSING

4 tablespoons extra virgin olive oil

juice of ½ -1 lemon

2 teaspoons Dijon mustard

1 clove garlic, very finely grated

salt and freshly cracked pepper

Place the quinoa into a medium saucepan with the water. Bring to the boil, reduce the heat, cover and simmer for 10 minutes until all the water is absorbed. Remove from the heat and leave to stand covered for 5 minutes then cool completely.

Mix all the dressing ingredients together in a large bowl and set aside.

Remove and discard the stalks from the kale, rinse the leaves and finely chop.

Add the kale and onion to the dressing and mix really well, as if you are rubbing and pressing the dressing and kale together. Set aside for about 10-15 minutes for the kale to soften.

Add the cooled quinoa, currants and pine nuts to the kale and gently toss to combine. If possible, prepare the salad in advance and leave to sit for 1-2 hours for all the flavours to combine.

Just before serving, cut the pomegranate in half and using the back of a wooden spoon, bash each half over the salad to release the fruit and collect the juice.

Transfer salad onto a serving platter. Crumble the feta over the salad, if using, and serve.

NOTE: THIS IS A VERY COLOURFUL SALAD, IDEAL TO SERVE ON SPECIAL OCCASIONS. I ALWAYS GETS COMMENTS ON HOW STUNNING THIS SALAD LOOKS ON THE TABLE, NOT TO MENTION HOW DELICIOUS IT TASTES.

PARSLEY, GARLIC AND LEMON CRUSTED LAMB

SERVES **4**

Preheat the oven to 400°F/200°C and line a baking tray with non-stick baking paper.

Place the oregano, parsley, garlic, lemon zest, juice and oil in a food processor and process using the pulse setting until all the ingredients are finely chopped.

Add the quinoa flakes, salt and pepper and process for a few seconds until everything is combined and resembles a paste.

Trim lamb of any excess fat and place on the baking tray, rub with a little extra virgin olive oil and season with salt and pepper. Roast in the oven for only 10 minutes.

After 10 minutes, remove the lamb from the oven and coat with the parsley mixture, pressing it down firmly.

Return lamb to the oven and roast for about 20 minutes until the lamb is cooked medium-well and the topping is golden. Lamb should be slightly pink inside, but adjust cooking time as per your preference.

Remove from the oven, cover with foil, and leave to rest for a good 10 minutes before slicing and serving.

1 teaspoon dried oregano
2 cups chopped parsley
3 cloves garlic
zest of 2 lemons
2 tablespoons lemon juice
1 teaspoon extra virgin olive oil
1 cup quinoa flakes
salt and freshly cracked pepper
2 racks of lamb made up of
  6-8 frenched lamb cutlets
  each
extra virgin olive oil, extra
salt and freshly cracked black
  pepper, extra

NOTE: THE NUMBER OF CUTLETS YOU PREPARE AND SERVE IS UP TO YOU. I USUALLY LIKE TO SERVE THREE TO FOUR CUTLETS PER PERSON DEPENDING ON THE APPETITES AT THE TABLE.

STICKY DATE PUDDINGS WITH CARAMEL SAUCE

MAKES 12 INDIVIDUAL PUDDINGS

1 lb oz/500 g dried dates
2½ cups water
1 teaspoon baking soda/
    bicarbonate of soda
9 oz/250 g unsalted butter
1¼ cups superfine/caster sugar
4 extra large eggs
2 teaspoons vanilla extract
1 teaspoon ground cinnamon
2 cups quinoa flour
2 teaspoons baking powder
strawberries, chopped, for
    garnish
vanilla ice-cream, for serving
    (optional)

CARAMEL SAUCE
8 oz/250 g unsalted butter
2 cups brown sugar
1 cup pouring cream
1 teaspoon vanilla bean paste
    or extract

Place dates and water into a medium to large saucepan and bring slowly to the boil, reduce the heat and simmer for 1 minute.

Remove from the heat, stir in the baking soda and set aside to cool completely.

The whole mixture will froth up when you add the soda so make sure you use a big enough saucepan so it doesn't spill over. Don't worry about all the liquid left as the date mixture will thicken as it cools.

Preheat the oven to 325°F/160°C. Grease 12 x 1 cup capacity tin moulds.

Using electric beaters cream the butter and sugar together until light and fluffy. Beat in the eggs one at a time with the vanilla and cinnamon.

Sift the flour and baking powder and slowly incorporate into the creamed butter mixture. Fold in the cooled dates and divide the cake mixture evenly between the prepared tins.

Place tins on a baking tray and bake for 35–40 minutes. When cooled, run a thin knife along the side of the moulds to loosen the puddings then invert onto a serving plate and serve with lots of caramel sauce and some chopped strawberries. And ice-cream, of course, if you wish.

To make the caramel sauce, place all ingredients into a small saucepan and simmer for a few minutes until the sauce starts to bubble and thicken.

NOTE: I PREFER TO MAKE THIS RECIPE AS LITTLE INDIVIDUAL PUDDINGS—THEY ARE A NICE SERVING SIZE. I HAVE ALWAYS DONE SO AS I LIKE THE LOOK OF THEM WHEN THEY ARE SERVED. ALSO THEY COOK A LOT QUICKER. YOU CAN MAKE ONE LARGE PUDDING IF YOU PREFER, JUST VARY THE COOKING TIME.

SPICY ITALIAN SAUSAGE WITH PEPPERS AND FENNEL

SERVES 4–6

Place the quinoa into a medium-sized saucepan with the water, bring to the boil, cover, reduce the heat and simmer for 10 minutes until all the water is absorbed. Remove from the heat and leave to stand, covered.

Remove the sausage meat from the casings. Roll the meat into little balls, and set aside in the fridge.

Cut the fennel bulbs in half and slice thickly. Reserve any of the green fronds as they will be used to garnish the dish.

Heat the oil in a large frying pan and cook the meatballs until browned and cooked. Remove from the pan and put to one side.

Add the onion to the pan and sauté until soft and golden, you may need to add a little more oil.

Add the fennel to the onions with the garlic, peppers, fennel seeds and chilli, and cook until the vegetables take on some colour and are tender but still firm.

Return the meat to the pan and season with salt and pepper, then stir in the quinoa and lemon juice if using. Gently mix together until the quinoa has combined with all the other ingredients.

Check and adjust seasoning if necessary and cook on low heat for about 5 minutes to heat everything through. Garnish with the fennel fronds and serve.

1½ cups quinoa, rinsed and drained
3 cups water
2 lb 4 oz/1 kg Italian sausages
2 bulbs baby fennel
2 tablespoons extra virgin olive oil
1 large onion, halved then sliced
3 cloves garlic, sliced
1 red bell pepper/capsicum, cut into pieces
1 green bell pepper/capsicum, cut into pieces
1 teaspoon fennel seeds
½ –1 teaspoon dried chilli flakes
salt and freshly cracked pepper
juice of ½ –1 lemon (optional)

NOTE: IF YOU ARE GLUTEN- /WHEAT-INTOLERANT, BE AWARE THAT SOME SAUSAGES ARE MADE WITH BREADCRUMBS OR CEREAL, OR BOTH.

STUFFED PEPPERS

SERVES 6

2 tablespoons extra virgin
    olive oil
1 large onion, finely chopped
1 lb/500 g ground/minced
    beef
1 tablespoon cumin seeds
2 cloves garlic, finely chopped
1 large fresh tomato, grated
1¼ cup quinoa, rinsed and
    drained
2 cups water
salt and freshly ground black
    pepper
handful chopped flat-leaf
    parsley
6 medium-large red or green
    bell peppers/capsicums
salt and freshly ground black
    pepper, to taste
handful flat-leaf parsley,
    chopped to serve

Heat the oil in a large frying pan and sauté the onion until soft and golden.

Add the beef, stir well and cook until lightly browned all over.

Stir in the cumin seeds and garlic, and cook for about 1-2 minutes until fragrant.

Add the tomato, quinoa, water and season with salt and pepper, bring to the boil, reduce the heat, cover and simmer for about 10 minutes or until all the water is absorbed. Stir the pan every now and then during the cooking time. Remove from the heat and stir through the parsley.

In the meantime, prepare the peppers. Preheat the oven to 400°F/200°C.

Cut the peppers in half lengthways then carefully remove all the seeds and membrane from inside.

Alternatively, you can cut a slice off the top of the bell peppers from the stalk end to make a lid then carefully remove all the seeds and membrane from inside.

Fill the peppers with the meat filling and place into a baking dish. Cover with their lid, if you have cut the bell peppers that way, drizzle with extra virgin and season with salt and pepper.

Bake for about 20-30 minutes until the peppers are slightly charred and cooked. Decorate with chopped parsley, just before serving.

NOTE: THESE ARE REALLY EASY TO MAKE AND ABSOLUTELY DELICIOUS. I OFTEN MAKE THEM FOR MY VEGETARIAN DAUGHTERS BY SUBSTITUTING THE MINCE WITH FINELY CHOPPED MUSHROOMS.

QUINOA

ZUCCHINI AND KALE SOUP

Thoroughly wash the kale, remove and discard the tough stalks. Chop the leaves and some of the more tender upper stalks very finely and set aside.

Heat the oil in a large saucepan and sauté onion until soft and translucent.

Stir in the garlic and cook for about 30 seconds until fragrant then stir in the kale, zucchini and quinoa.

Pour in the stock and season with salt and a good grind of pepper.

Bring to the boil, reduce the heat, cover and simmer for about 30-40 minutes until the quinoa is cooked and tender. Remove the soup from the heat and leave to sit for about 10-15 minutes before serving.

Serve with a drizzle of extra virgin olive oil, a good grind of black pepper and a dollop of sour cream if using and shavings of parmesan cheese.

6 large kale stalks
2 tablespoons extra virgin olive oil
1 large onion, finely chopped
3 cloves garlic, finely grated
21 oz/600 g zucchini, coarsely grated
⅔ cup red quinoa, rinsed and drained
9 cups hot chicken or vegetable stock
salt to taste
freshly cracked black pepper
low-fat sour cream (optional)
shaved parmesan cheese, for serving

NOTE: THIS IS A THICK AND FILLING SOUP. EXTRA STOCK OR WATER CAN BE ADDED IF YOU PREFER A THINNER SOUP.

AMARANTH

Amaranth is a very old grain that originated in South America and has been around for over 7000 years. It is making a big comeback and is increasing in popularity due to the health benefits associated with this little seed.

It was considered one of the most important crops and the staple food for the Aztecs, Incas and Mayans. The Aztecs also believed that amaranth gave them supernatural powers and were known to refer to it as the 'food of immortality'. Amaranth was not used only as food by the Aztecs, it was also used in religious rituals, which led to the Spaniards banning its cultivation.

The word amaranth comes from the Greek word *amarantos* meaning everlasting. It was banned for a number of centuries but it could never be completely eradicated so it would seem that it was very appropriately named. Amaranth, like quinoa, belongs to the goosefoot family and is distantly related to spinach. Also, like quinoa, amaranth is a seed but is commonly referred to as a grain.

Amaranth is grown extensively in many parts of the world and not just in South America. It is now also grown in the USA, China, Russia, India and the Czech Republic as well as other parts of the world.

Gluten- and wheat-free, amaranth is an excellent food for those suffering with coeliac disease. It is also suitable for people with diabetes as it is considered to be a low GI food. High in fibre and with a slightly lower carbohydrate content to other similar grains, this tiny seed is very powerful.

Amaranth has numerous health benefits, as it is packed with vitamins and minerals. It contains a very large quantity of protein and, unlike most other grains except quinoa, contains the very important amino acid lysine. Lysine is important for tissue repair and growth. Amaranth is a rich source of phytosterols, which have properties that can help reduce cholesterol.

Amaranth is also high in B vitamins, iron, calcium, magnesium, manganese, potassium, phosphorus and vitamin E, and is believed to be the only grain that contains vitamin C. It has been described as having a nutty taste, however, I find the taste to be quite earthy with strong spinach-tasting overtones.

How to use amaranth

Amaranth comes in grain, flour, flake and puffed form. It can be used in many ways but possibly the easiest to work with and the most popular would be flaked and puffed amaranth.

The whole grain tends to become rather gluggy and sticky once cooked and it is not at its best when used on its own. Add the whole grain to soups or use it to make porridge. A small amount of amaranth mixed in with other grains can work well in some dishes.

Amaranth flour can be used in breads, cereal, cookies, pancakes and other flour-based cooking, or it can be used on its own as the flour base in some gluten- or wheat-free baking. It should also be noted that, depending on the different brands, some flours can be quite 'grainy', and not very finely ground. The flour does not contain a raising agent.

Flaked amaranth is great to use as a stuffing and crumbing ingredient and in porridges.

Puffed amaranth is the easiest to work with and has the mildest taste of the four. It can be used to make cakes, slices, biscuits, muesli and other baked products.

AMARANTH, CASHEW, GINGER AND CRANBERRY BITES

MAKES 24 BALLS

3½ oz/100 g raw cashews
2 oz/60 g glacé ginger
2½ oz/80 g dried apricots
2 oz/60 g dried cranberries
2 oz /60 g golden raisins/
  sultana
2 tablespoons organic raw
  coconut oil
1 cup puffed amaranth

Place cashews in a food processor and process until finely chopped. Add the ginger, apricots, cranberries, raisins and coconut oil, and continue processing until the nuts and fruit are finely chopped and you have a slightly sticky mixture with a little texture to it.

Transfer this mixture into a bowl and add the amaranth puffs. Mix all the ingredients together; your hands are probably the best tool for this. Press the mixture as you mix so that it holds firmly together.

Roll the mixture into bite-sized rounds or a size that best suits you, and refrigerate until set. These bites will keep in the refrigerator for at least 3-4 weeks. I prefer to take out them out of the fridge and serve at room temperature.

NOTE: RAW ORGANIC COCONUT OIL IS ALSO CONSIDERED TO BE A SUPERFOOD.

LITTLE AMARANTH CAKES WITH CRANBERRIES AND ORANGE

MAKES 12

4 oz/125 g almond meal
1 cup pure confectioners'/icing
  sugar, sifted
½ cup amaranth flour
½ teaspoon gluten-free baking
  powder
4 oz/125 g dried cranberries
2 teaspoons orange zest
2 tablespoons orange juice
4 oz/125 g unsalted butter,
  melted and cooled
½ teaspoon vanilla extract
4 large egg whites

ORANGE ICING
½ cup sifted confectioner's/
  icing sugar
1 tablespoon orange juice

Preheat the oven to 325°F/170°C. Grease 12 ovenproof tea cups or line a 12-cup muffin tin with paper cases.

Place the almond meal, confectioner's sugar, amaranth flour and baking powder into a bowl and use a whisk to mix well, breaking up any lumps of mixture that may have formed.

Mix in the cranberries and orange zest, then lightly stir in the orange juice, butter and vanilla.

Beat the egg whites until foamy and soft peaks form, then gently fold into the mixture. Spoon the mixture evenly into the prepared tea cups or muffin tins.

Bake for about 20 minutes until golden brown and cooked when tested with a metal skewer.

Remove from the oven and cool completely before drizzling with the orange icing.

To make the icing, mix the confectioner's sugar with as much of the orange juice needed to make a slightly thick but runny consistency.

NOTE: THE TASTE COMBINATION OF DRIED CRANBERRIES AND ORANGE IS REALLY LOVELY. THESE LITTLE CAKES ARE QUITE MOIST AND DELICIOUS AND A REAL HIT.

APPLE, RAISIN AND CINNAMON PORRIDGE

SERVES 4

1 large apple
½ cup amaranth grain
½ cup amaranth flakes
2 cups water
½ cup golden raisins/sultanas
1 teaspoon vanilla bean paste
  or extract
½ –1 teaspoon ground
  cinnamon
½ cup milk
2-3 tablespoons maple syrup
milk, for serving
strawberries, for serving

Coarsely grate the unpeeled apple and place into a medium-sized saucepan with the amaranth grain, flakes and water, mix well.

Add the raisins, vanilla and cinnamon, bring to the boil, reduce the heat, cover and simmer on low heat for 20-25 minutes until the grains are cooked and all the water is absorbed.

When cooked to a soft consistency that you prefer, remove from the heat, stir in the milk and sweeten to taste with the maple syrup or sweetener of your choice.

Return to the heat for a few minutes to thicken a little more.

Serve warm with extra milk if you think necessary and sliced fresh strawberries or berries of your choice.

NOTE: AS THIS PORRIDGE USES AMARANTH AND ONLY AMARANTH AS THE MAIN INGREDIENT, YOU WILL FIND THAT THE LOVELY AND NATURAL TASTE OF THE AMARANTH REALLY STANDS OUT. I HAVE PURPOSELY NOT MIXED IN ANY OTHER 'CEREAL' OR 'GRAIN' SO THAT THE TRUE TASTE OF THIS VERY NUTRITIONAL GRAIN CAN BE FULLY ENJOYED AND APPRECIATED.

AMARANTH PORRIDGE WITH PEARS, ORANGE AND CINNAMON

SERVES 4

Place pears, orange juice and zest into a saucepan with the sugar. Bring to the boil, reduce the heat and simmer for about 5 minutes until pears are tender. Set aside.

Place amaranth, water, milk and vanilla into a medium non-stick saucepan, bring to the boil, reduce the heat, cover and simmer for about 30-40 minutes until amaranth is cooked and soft.

Stir the pan every now and then to prevent the milk solids from sticking to the bottom of the pan.

When the porridge is cooked, stir in the honey and as much of the cinnamon as you like. Fold the pear mixture through the porridge and serve.

You can hold back some of the pear mixture and use it as a garnish when serving the porridge.

4 pears, peeled and diced
juice and zest of 2 oranges
1-2 tablespoons raw sugar
1 cup amaranth grain
1 cup water
2 cups low-fat milk
1 teaspoon vanilla extract
2 tablespoons honey
½ -1 teaspoon ground
  cinnamon

NOTE: CINNAMON IS A REALLY NICE SPICE TO USE IN THIS RECIPE BUT YOU CAN USE NUTMEG OR CARDAMOM IF YOU PREFER, JUST ADD LESS THAN THE AMOUNT SPECIFIED FOR CINNAMON ABOVE. YOU CAN ALSO REPLACE THE HONEY WITH MAPLE SYRUP. AVOID USING OVER-RIPE PEARS FOR THIS RECIPE.

HERBED MEATBALLS

Place the amaranth flakes and beef into a large bowl with the onion, garlic, mint, parsley, chives, salt and pepper. Mix well to thoroughly combine.

Shape the mince mixture into balls the size of a walnut and lightly dust with the flour.

Heat the oil in a large frying pan over medium heat until hot and shallow fry the meat balls until golden, about 3-5 minutes each side.

Serve hot or cold.

½ cup amaranth flakes
1 lb/500 g ground/minced beef
1 medium onion, grated
2 cloves garlic, grated
4 tablespoons finely chopped fresh mint
3 tablespoons finely chopped flat leaf parsley
2 tablespoons finely chopped fresh chives
salt and freshly cracked black pepper
amaranth flour, for dusting
olive oil, for cooking

NOTE: THESE MEATBALLS ARE LOVELY SERVED HOT, WARM OR COLD. THEY ARE GREAT FOR PICNICS OR ON SANDWICHES AND ABSOLUTELY DELICIOUS SERVED WITH A DOLLOP OF HUMMUS OR MINTED YOGHURT. I LIKE TO SERVE THESE AS A KEBAB.

AMARANTH, QUINOA, DATE AND GINGER BISCUITS

MAKES ABOUT 20

- 4 oz/125 g unsalted butter, softened
- 1 tablespoon light brown sugar
- ¼ cup superfine/caster sugar
- 1 extra large egg
- 1 teaspoon vanilla bean paste
- ¾ cup quinoa flour
- 1 teaspoon gluten-free baking powder
- 4 oz/125 g dried dates, chopped
- 2 oz/60 g glacé ginger, chopped
- 2 cups puffed amaranth
- 1 tablespoon orange juice

Preheat the oven to 180°C/350°F and line two large baking trays with non-stick baking paper.

Cream the butter with the brown and caster sugar until light and creamy, then mix in the egg and vanilla.

Sift the quinoa flour with the baking powder and fold into the creamed butter mixture.

Using a spatula, mix in the dates, ginger, amaranth puffs and the orange juice. The mixture may seem a little dry but don't be tempted to add more liquid just press together as you are mixing so that it holds.

Place spoonfuls of the mixture onto the prepared trays and bake for 10-12 minutes until golden.

Leave to cool slightly in trays before transferring to a cooling rack to cool completely.

NOTE: THIS BISCUIT RECIPE USES TWO SUPERFOODS TO MAKE THESE BISCUITS. MY HUSBAND LOVES THESE BUT, BEING A HUGE GINGER FAN, HE PREFERS THEM WITH TWICE THE AMOUNT OF GINGER IN THEM.

BLACK BEAN AND SWEET POTATO SOUP WITH AMARANTH

SERVES 6–8

Heat the oil in a large saucepan and sauté onion and celery until soft.

Stir in the garlic, turmeric, chillies, cumin and cilantro, and cook for about 1 minute until fragrant.

Add the sweet potato, stock and amaranth and season with salt to taste, keeping in mind the saltiness of the stock and the sweetness of the potato.

Bring to the boil, reduce the heat, cover and simmer on low-medium heat for about 30 minutes until the potato and amaranth are cooked and the soup has thickened.

Add the beans and cook for another 10 minutes. If you find the soup is too thick, add a little more stock or water. Stir through the lime juice and cilantro and serve with a dollop of Greek yoghurt.

NOTE: FRESH TURMERIC IS READILY AVAILABLE AT MOST GREENGROCERS AND SUPERMARKETS. IT IS A REALLY LOVELY INGREDIENT TO HAVE ON HAND TO USE IN ANY DISH THAT REQUIRES TURMERIC, ESPECIALLY CURRIES. IF YOU ARE UNABLE TO FIND IT, THEN SUBSTITUTE 1 TEASPOON OF GROUND TURMERIC. TURMERIC IS KNOWN TO BE VERY HIGH IN ANTI-OXIDANTS. I TEND TO KEEP MY FRESH TURMERIC IN THE FREEZER IF I FIND THAT I HAVE TOO MUCH OF IT. IT KEEPS WELL AND YOU CAN GRATE IT INTO WHATEVER YOU ARE COOKING DIRECTLY FROM THE FREEZER. IT WILL PEEL EASILY AS YOU ARE GRATING.

2 tablespoons extra virgin olive oil
1 large onion, finely chopped
1 stick celery, finely diced
2 cloves garlic, finely chopped
1 tablespoon grated fresh turmeric
1-2 long red chillies, de-seeded and chopped
1 teaspoon ground cumin
1 teaspoon ground coriander
2 lb 4 oz/1 kg kumera/orange sweet potato, peeled and coarsely grated
8 cups hot vegetable stock
½ cup amaranth grain
salt
2 x 14 oz/400 g cans black beans, drained
juice of ½ a lime
small handful of fresh cilantro/ coriander, chopped
unsweetened Greek yoghurt, for serving (optional)

COCONUT AND VEGETABLE SOUP WITH AMARANTH

SERVES 4–6

1–2 tablespoons extra virgin
    olive oil
1 large onion, finely chopped
2 medium carrots, diced
2 stalks celery, diced
2 cloves garlic, finely chopped
1 tablespoon grated fresh
    turmeric
1 teaspoon curry powder
⅔ cup amaranth grain
6 cups hot vegetable or
    chicken stock
salt and freshly cracked black
    pepper
1 x 14 oz/400 g can low-fat
    coconut milk
2 cups frozen peas
1 cup frozen corn
juice of 1 lime or lemon, for
    serving
fresh cilantro/coriander leaves,
    for garnish

Heat the oil in a large saucepan and sauté the onion, carrots and celery until tender.

Stir in the garlic, turmeric and curry powder and cook for about 1 minute, then add the amaranth, stock and season with salt and pepper, keeping in mind that the stock may be salty.

Bring to the boil, reduce the heat, cover and simmer on low-medium heat for about 30 minutes until the amaranth is soft and soup has thickened.

Add the coconut milk, peas and corn, bring back to the boil and simmer for another 10 minutes.

Serve with lime or lemon juice squeezed over and fresh cilantro leaves.

NOTE: IF YOU ARE UNABLE TO FIND FRESH TUMERIC, THEN SUBSTITUTE IT WITH 1 TEASPOON OF GROUND TURMERIC. TURMERIC IS KNOWN TO BE VERY HIGH IN ANTIOXIDANTS. I TEND TO KEEP MY FRESH TURMERIC IN THE FREEZER IF I FIND THAT I HAVE TOO MUCH OF IT. IT KEEPS WELL AND YOU CAN GRATE IT INTO WHATEVER YOU ARE COOKING DIRECTLY FROM THE FREEZER. IT WILL PEEL EASILY AS YOU ARE GRATING.

HERBED CRUMBED FISH FILLETS

SERVES 4

Combine the amaranth flakes with the garlic, lemon zest, chives, parsley, coriander, chilli, and salt and pepper.

Mix well, making sure you rub the garlic through the flakes so that it is evenly distributed.

Lightly dust the fish with the flour then dip into the beaten egg and then press into the flake mixture. Cover the fish completely with the flake mixture, pressing firmly.

Heat the oil in a large frying pan on medium heat until hot and gently shallow fry the fillets until cooked and golden, approximately 3-5 minutes each side depending on the thickness of the fish.

Remove from the pan onto kitchen paper, then serve hot with a good squeeze of lemon or lime juice.

1 cup amaranth flakes
1 large clove garlic, finely grated
zest of 1 lemon
1 tablespoon chopped fresh chives
1 tablespoon chopped fresh flat leaf parsley
1 tablespoon chopped fresh cilantro/coriander
½ -1 teaspoon chilli flakes
salt and freshly cracked black pepper
4 fish fillets
amaranth flour, for dusting
1 extra large egg, lightly beaten
olive oil, for shallow frying
lemon or lime juice for serving

NOTE: CHOOSE WHICHEVER FISH FILLETS YOU PREFER. A WHITE BONELESS FISH SUCH AS DORY WORKS WELL IN THIS RECIPE.

LEMON AND PISTACHIO AMARANTH MUFFINS

MAKES 12

Preheat the oven to 325°F/ 170°C. Line a 12-cup muffin tin with paper cases.

Place the almond meal into a large bowl then sift in the icing sugar, amaranth flour and baking powder, and mix well to combine.

Mix in the lemon zest and juice, then lightly stir in the pistachio nuts, butter and vanilla.

Beat the egg whites until foamy and soft peaks form then gently fold into the mixture.

Spoon the mixture evenly into the prepared tins.

Bake for approximately 20 minutes until golden brown and cooked when tested with a metal skewer.

4 oz/125 g almond meal
1 cup confectioner's/icing sugar, sifted
⅔ cup amaranth flour
1 teaspoon gluten-free baking powder
zest of 1 lemon
2 tablespoons lemon juice
4 oz/125 g pistachio nuts, finely chopped
4 oz/125 g unsalted butter, melted and cooled
1 teaspoon vanilla extract
4 large egg whites

NOTE: THE COMBINATION OF LEMON AND PISTACHIOS GIVES A LOVELY FLAVOUR TO THESE MUFFINS. SOME FLOURS ARE NOT GROUND AS FINE AS OTHERS RESULTING IN A 'GRAINY' TEXTURE.

CHIA

Chia is an ancient seed dating back centuries. Native to South America, it is another powerful superfood that has been a very important part of the Aztec and Mayan diet for centuries, as it was highly valued as a staple food along with beans and corn. It is not only known for its nutritional value but also for its medicinal benefits.

Chia, a tiny nutrient-dense edible seed, is a member of the mint family and originally came from Southern Mexico from a plant called *Salvia hispanica* where it grew in abundance. Chia is the Mayan word for 'strength' and the seeds were used to sustain the Aztec warriors during their time of conquest, as it was considered food that increased stamina.

Chia seeds are considered to be energy boosters, and a food that increases stamina and performance, and can raise the level of endurance. It was believed that 1 tablespoon of chia seeds was enough to fuel an individual's body for 24 hours. Chia was also used to stimulate saliva and relieve skin conditions and joint pain. The seeds were held in such high regard that they were also used as currency.

Chia is a whole grain, so eating it on a regular basis can lessen their risk of developing heart disease, diabetes and bowel cancer. It can also help with weight control as the seeds expand once consumed, curbing hunger.

The chia seed is gluten-free and the richest vegetarian source of omega-3, more so than any other food. It is also an excellent source of fibre and loaded with antioxidants, as well as an impressive range of B vitamins. Chia seeds also contain calcium, iron, magnesium, phosphorus, niacin and zinc.

Chia seeds are a valuable source of antioxidants, which help the body fight off disease. They are high in soluble fibre, which can help reduce blood pressure, blood sugar levels and blood clotting. They are also effective in lowering cholesterol.

The massive amount of omega-3 fatty acids found in chia seeds can have an anti-inflammatory effect and also help support our cardiovascular system as well as our immune, nervous and reproductive systems.

Chia seeds have a mild nutty flavour and can be eaten and digested as a whole grain. They can be purchased as black or white seeds, and are readily available in major supermarkets and all health food stores, as well as some greengrocers.

Uses for chia seeds

They have many uses in cooking: they can be sprinkled over your cereal, yoghurt, stir-fries or salads, or cooked in your porridge. In fact chia seeds can be sprinkled over just about any food.

They can be added to soups, casseroles, baked foods or batters, such as breads, cakes, muffins and pancakes, or to thicken gravies. They are excellent when blitzed into smoothies and make excellent puddings that are very easy to prepare.

When they are unsoaked they are quite hard and crunchy, but when they are added to water they soften and can absorb up to 12 times their weight, making them more palatable to some people.

The minute that chia seeds come into contact with liquid or moisture they start to soften and absorb moisture, turning them quite gelatinous.

BAKED POTATOES WITH CHIA DUKKHA AND SOUR CREAM

SERVES 4–6

2 oz/60 g hazelnuts, skinned
2 oz/60 g pine nuts
2 tablespoons coriander seeds
2 tablespoons sesame seeds
¼ cup chia seeds
1 teaspoon ground cumin
½ –1 teaspoon ground chilli
1½ teaspoons sea salt
½ teaspoon freshly cracked
 black pepper
⅛ teaspoon cinnamon
pinch of nutmeg
1-2 tablespoons sesame seeds,
 extra
4 or 6 whole potatoes
sour cream or Greek yoghurt,
 to serve
chopped fresh chives or
 scallions/shallots

In a non-stick frying pan, dry roast the hazelnuts for about 2 minutes until they start to change colour.

Add the pine nuts to the pan and continue dry roasting until they start to change colour, then add the coriander seeds, sesame and chia seeds and continue dry-roasting for another 2-3 minutes until fragrant, tossing regularly so that the nuts and seeds do not burn.

Remove from the pan and place into a food processor with the cumin, chilli, salt, pepper, cinnamon and nutmeg and process until the mixture is ground to a fine mix.

After the spice mix has been through the food processor, dry-roast the extra sesame seeds until just golden, cool and toss through the blended mix.

Preheat the oven to 400°F/200°C.

Wash and scrub the potatoes and bake in the oven with the skin on until soft and tender when tested with a metal skewer.

When the potatoes are cooked, make four incisions across the top of each one, without cutting right through, and gently squeeze so as to expose the creamy soft potato flesh.

Mix some of the spice mixture into the sour cream or yoghurt and place a thick dollop into the centre of each potato, then sprinkle the top with more of the dukkha mix and top with chives or scallions. Delicious.

NOTE: ANY LEFTOVER COOLED DUKKHA MIXTURE CAN BE STORED IN YOUR PANTRY IN A JAR WITH A TIGHT-FITTING LID. IT KEEPS REALLY WELL FOR A FEW WEEKS. I OFTEN MAKE A BATCH AND KEEP IT IN MY PANTRY READY TO USE WHEN NEEDED.

CHIA AND AMARANTH ZUCCHINI MINT FRITTERS

MAKES 10–12 FRITTERS

13 oz/375 g zucchini/
  courgettes
1 long red chilli
4 scallions/spring onions, thinly
  sliced
2 large eggs, lightly beaten
2 tablespoons finely chopped
  mint
1-2 cloves garlic, finely grated
1 teaspoon ground cumin
2 tablespoons chia seeds
salt and freshly ground black
  pepper
½ cup amaranth flour
olive oil for shallow frying
1 cup Greek yoghurt
1-2 tablespoons finely chopped
  fresh mint (extra)

Top and tail the zucchinis then coarsely grate and place in a large bowl.

De-seed or leave the seeds in the chilli if you wish and finely chop.

Add the chilli to the zucchini with the scallions, eggs, mint, garlic, cumin, chia, salt and pepper. Stir in the flour and mix to combine.

Heat the oil in a frying pan until medium-hot, drop spoonfuls of the zucchini mixture into the oil and cook until golden on both sides about 2-3 minutes. It is best not to overcrowd the pan.

Remove from the pan with a slotted spoon and drain on kitchen paper.

Mix the yoghurt and extra mint together and serve the patties with a sprinkle of sea salt flakes and a dollop of the yoghurt.

NOTE: THIS IS ANOTHER RECIPE THAT USES MORE THAN ONE SUPERFOODS. THESE ARE BEST EATEN HOT WHEN FIRST MADE. HOWEVER, ANY LEFTOVERS CAN BE EATEN COLD AND ARE DELICIOUS IN A SANDWICH WITH A GOOD CHUTNEY.

CHIA, GARLIC AND CHILLI CHICKEN WINGS

Soak the saffron strands in the boiling water for about 5 minutes.

Using a sharp knife or poultry shears, separate the wings into three pieces, discard the tip (or save them for stock) and place the other two parts of the wing into a bowl.

Mix together the saffron water, oil, garlic, ginger, paprika, chillies, salt and pepper.

Coat the wings with the mixture and leave to marinate for about 1 hour. Sprinkle the chia seeds over the chicken and mix well so that all the wings are well coated with the chia seeds.

Preheat the oven to 375°F/190°C and line a large baking tray with non-stick baking paper.

Place the wings in a single layer on the baking tray and bake for about 20 minutes each side until they are cooked and a deep golden colour.

Squeeze the lime juice over the wings and serve while hot.

½ teaspoon saffron strands
2 teaspoons boiling water
12 large chicken wings
2 teaspoons olive oil
3 cloves garlic, finely grated
1 teaspoon finely grated ginger
½ teaspoon ground sweet paprika
2 long red chillies, de-seeded and chopped
salt
freshly ground black pepper (optional)
2–3 tablespoons chia seeds
lime juice

NOTE: YOU CAN VARY THE AMOUNT OF CHIA SEEDS AND CHILLIES USED IN THIS DISH. THE CHIA SEEDS ADD A REAL CRUNCH, WHICH IS DELICIOUS.

SMOOTHIES

BANANA AND HONEY
2½ cups almond milk
2 tablespoons chia seeds
1 large ripe banana
2 tablespoons honey
1-2 teaspoons organic raw
    extra virgin coconut oil
    (optional)
1 teaspoon vanilla bean paste
ice cubes

CHOCOLATE ALMOND
2 cups icy cold almond milk
1 large banana
1½ tablespoons chia seeds
1 tablespoon pure raw cacao
    powder
1 tablespoon quinoa flakes
¼ teaspoon ground cinnamon
⅛ teaspoon ground nutmeg
2 tablespoons honey
ice cubes

MIXED BERRY
1-2 teaspoons organic raw
    coconut oil
1½ cups coconut water
a few sprigs of mint
2 tablespoons honey
ice cubes
2 cups frozen berries
2 tablespoons chia seeds

For each recipe, place all of the ingredients into a blender and blend until thick, smooth and creamy. Vary the sweetener to suit your taste and serve immediately.

These are filling smoothies and should keep you going for a few hours.

NOTE: RAW ORGANIC EXTRA VIRGIN COCONUT OIL IS ALSO CONSIDERED TO BE A SUPERFOOD AND THIS IS A GOOD WAY TO INCLUDE IT IN THE EVERYDAY DIET. YOU CAN LEAVE IT OUT IF YOU WISH.

CHIA BANANA BREAD

Preheat the oven to 325°F/170°C and lightly grease a 9 in/24 cm loaf tin.

Stir the lemon juice and rind through the mashed bananas and set aside.

Cream the butter and sugar together with electric beaters until light and creamy.

Beat in the eggs one at a time, and then fold in the almond meal.

Sift the flour and fold into the mixture with the chia seeds, bananas, milk, vanilla and walnuts if used.

Pour the mixture into the prepared tin and bake for about 50-55 minutes or until a skewer comes out clean when inserted.

Cool in the tin for about 15 minutes before turning out on to wire rack.

3 large ripe bananas, mashed
1 tablespoon lemon juice
1 teaspoon lemon rind
4 oz/125 g butter at room temperature
1 cup loosely packed brown sugar
2 large eggs
½ cup almond meal
1½ cups self-raising flour
3 tablespoons black chia seeds
⅓ cup milk
1 teaspoon vanilla extract
3 oz/90 g chopped walnuts (optional)

NOTE: THIS CAKE IS DELICIOUS WHEN TOASTED.

CHICKEN STIR-FRY WITH SNOW PEAS

SERVES 4

1 tablespoon chia seeds

3 tablespoons water

3 tablespoons soy sauce

2 tablespoons shao-xing wine

24 oz/750 g chicken breast fillets, trimmed and sliced thinly

2-3 cloves garlic, finely chopped

1 thumb-sized knob of ginger, grated

1 tablespoon oil

½ teaspoon sesame oil

1 red chilli, sliced

4 scallions/spring onions, sliced diagonally

6 oz/180 g snow peas, string removed

Soak the chia seeds in the water for 5 minutes until it thickens, then mix in 2 tablespoons of soy sauce and shao-xing wine and leave to stand for 5 minutes until the mixture thickens.

Place the chicken in a bowl with the garlic, ginger and remaining soy sauce. Mix and allow to marinate for about 5 minutes.

Heat the oils in a wok or large frying pan until hot, add the chicken and stir-fry over high heat for 7-9 minutes until almost cooked and golden. You may need to do this in batches.

When all the chicken is ready, stir in the chilli, scallions and snow peas, and stir-fry for another 2-3 minutes or until the peas are tender but still crisp.

Stir in the chia and soy sauce mixture and keep stirring for 1-2 minutes until all the flavours combine.

Serve with steamed rice or with some noodles stirred through.

NOTE: THE CHIA SEEDS ADD A LOVELY CRUNCH TO THIS DISH. THIS IS NOT MEANT TO BE A STIR-FRY WITH LOTS OF SAUCE. IF YOU FEEL THE STIR-FRY IS TOO DRY THEN JUST ADD A LITTLE MORE WATER .

CHIA

COCONUT, MANGO AND CHIA PUDDING

SERVES 2

1 x 14 oz/400 g can low-fat
  coconut milk
½ cup coconut water
½ cup chia seeds
1-2 tablespoons honey or
  maple syrup
1 mango

Place the coconut milk, coconut water, chia seeds and sweetener into a bowl and stir vigorously.

Leave to stand for about 15 minutes, stirring a few times during that time.

Peel and cut the mango into cubes, reserve some to use as a garnish, and stir the remainder into the coconut mixture.

Squeeze the skin and the seed of the mango over the pudding and mix in whatever juice you manage to collect.

Cover and refrigerate for at least 2 hours so that the pudding chills and sets. The longer the pudding sits in the fridge the more intense the flavour of the mango and the creamier the pudding.

Adjust the amount of coconut water you add to the pudding to suit your taste and the texture you prefer.

Serve garnished with the reserved pieces of mango.

NOTE: IF YOU PREFER A SMOOTHER CONSISTENCY WITHOUT THE SEEDS BEING SO OBVIOUS, THEN PLACE THE MILK, WATER, CHIA SEEDS AND SWEETENER INTO A BLENDER, BLEND UNTIL SMOOTH THEN FOLD IN THE MANGO AND REFRIGERATE.

YOU CAN USE PIECES OF FRESH PINEAPPLE OR FRESH BANANA INSTEAD OF THE MANGO OR FOR A TROPICAL TREAT USE ALL THREE.

CREAMY COFFEE AND ORANGE CHIA PUDDING

Dissolve the sugar in the coffee then add the chia seeds and stir quite briskly with a fork.

Leave the seeds to stand and soak for about 10-15 minutes, stirring every now then so that the seeds don't sink to the bottom.

Stir in the milk, vanilla and orange zest, mix well and leave to stand another 5 minutes.

Refrigerate for at least 2 hours before serving garnished with fresh orange segments and flaked almonds.

Segment the orange by cutting the top and bottom of the orange with a sharp knife. Then carefully remove the skin away from the flesh using downward cutting stokes and discard the skin. Do this over a bowl so that you can collect the juices which you can stir into the pudding before serving.

Remove any white pith that may have been left behind then cut between each membrane to release the orange flesh in segments.

1 cup hot double shot coffee
2 tablespoons sugar or sweetener of choice
5 tablespoons chia seeds
½ cup low fat or almond milk
1 teaspoon vanilla bean paste or extract
zest of 1 orange
1 orange, segmented
flaked almonds, for garnish

NOTE: FOR A THICKER CONSISTENCY USE MORE CHIA SEEDS. YOU CAN SEGMENT THE ORANGE THAT WAS USED FOR ZESTING WHEN MAKING THE PUDDING. JUST EXERCISE EXTRA CARE WHEN CUTTING INTO IT.

GARLIC AND CHIA MUSHROOMS

SERVES 2—4

1 lb/500 g mushrooms
3 tablespoons olive oil
1-2 long red chillies
3-4 cloves garlic, finely
    chopped
salt and freshly ground black
    pepper
½ cup chopped fresh flat-leaf
    parsley
2 tablespoons chia seeds
extra chopped parsley, to
    garnish

Wipe mushrooms with a slightly damp cloth to remove any dirt, then slice thinly.

Heat the oil in a large frying pan, add the mushrooms and cook until they are tender.

Slice the chillies with or without the seeds and add them to the mushrooms with the garlic and cook for 1-2 minutes, until fragrant, then season with salt and pepper.

Stir in the parsley and chia seeds and cook for another 1-2 minutes.

Sprinkle with extra parsley and serve.

NOTE: THIS DISH CAN BE USED AS A SIDE DISH WITH MEAT, FISH OR CHICKEN, OR AS A MAIN MEAL SERVED WITH SOME RICE.

SPICED CHIA AND HONEYED ROASTED NUTS

Preheat the oven to 325°F/ 160°C and line a large baking tray with non-stick baking paper.

Mix the chia seeds, sea salt, garlic salt, paprika, cumin, and cayenne pepper together and set aside.

Place the nuts in a bowl with the coconut oil and honey and mix well to thoroughly coat the nuts with the honey and oil.

Sprinkle the spice mixture over the nuts and toss well until the nuts are completely coated with the spice mixture.

Place in a single layer on the baking tray and roast for about 10-15 minutes until they are golden and roasted. Keep an eye on them as they can burn easily.

Remove from the oven and carefully move the baking paper with the nuts off the tray and onto a cool surface, this stops the cooking process and allows them to cool more quickly.

Using a spatula, keep tossing and mixing the nuts so the spice mixture sticks to them and they separate as they cool.

Cool completely, then store in an airtight container; they will keep for a few weeks. If they stick together just give the container a good shake.

2½ tablespoons chia seeds
1 teaspoon sea salt
1 teaspoon garlic salt
1 teaspoon ground paprika
2 teaspoons ground cumin
½ -1 teaspoon cayenne pepper
1 lb/500 g raw nuts of your choice
1 tablespoon organic raw coconut oil
3 tablespoons runny honey

NOTE: THESE ARE GREAT TO HAVE ON HAND AND PULL OUT WHENEVER YOU NEED SOMETHING SPECIAL AND DIFFERENT. I USUALLY LIKE TO USE A COMBINATION OF CASHEWS, ALMONDS, HAZELNUTS, MACADAMIA AND BRAZIL NUTS.

KALE AND CHIA SMOOTHIE

SERVES 2

2 large kale leaves
1 banana, peeled and sliced
2 stalks celery, roughly
    chopped
9 fl oz/250 ml pure apple juice
1-2 tablespoons chia seeds
2 teaspoons honey
1 Lebanese cucumber, sliced
4-5 mint leaves
1 cup ice cubes

Remove and discard the tough stalks of the kale, wash well and roughly chop the leaves.

Add to a blender with all the other ingredients and blend until really smooth.

Serve immediately.

This smoothie should be prepared just before serving and drunk straight after before it starts to lose its vibrant green colour.

You can adjust the amount of chia seeds used and add more or less as you wish.

NOTE: THIS IS A REALLY FRESH-TASTING SMOOTHIE—SIMPLY DELICIOUS. YOU CAN SUBSTITUTE THE APPLE JUICE WITH COCONUT WATER IF YOU LIKE. I SOMETIMES LIKE TO ADD A SQUEEZE OF LEMON OR LIME JUICE AS WELL.

MOROCCAN CHICKEN PATTIES

SERVES 6

Place the chicken mince into a large bowl with the onion, garlic, cumin, coriander, paprika, ginger, cinnamon and chilli flakes. Mix well until thoroughly combined.

Mix in the chia seeds and fresh cilantro, and season with salt to taste.

Mix well then divide the chicken mixture into 12 and shape into patties.

Heat enough oil to shallow fry the patties in a large frying pan over medium heat and cook until golden on both sides and cooked through.

Remove from the heat and drain on kitchen paper.

Serve hot with a squeeze of lemon juice and garnished with coriander leaves and sweet chilli sauce. You can also serve with a dollop of unsweetened Greek yoghurt.

2 lb 4 oz/1 kg chicken mince
1 onion, grated
2-3 cloves garlic, grated
1½ teaspoons ground cumin
1 teaspoon ground coriander
1 teaspoon paprika
1 teaspoon ground ginger
¼ teaspoon cinnamon
½ -1 teaspoon chilli flakes
3 tablespoons black chia seeds
2-3 tablespoons finely chopped
   fresh cilantro/coriander
salt
olive oil, for frying
lemon wedges, for serving
cilantro/coriander leaves, for
   garnish
sweet chilli sauce, for serving

NOTE: THESE PATTIES CAN ALSO BE PREPARED USING LAMB OR BEEF MINCE. LEFTOVER PATTIES, IF THERE ARE ANY, MAKE GREAT SANDWICH FILLINGS AND ARE DELICIOUS ON BUNS AS HAMBURGER FILLING.

POMEGRANATE AND CHIA PUDDING

SERVES 2—4

1 large pomegranate
2 cups pomegranate juice
6 tablespoons black chia seeds
thick, plain Greek yoghurt, for
 garnish

Cut the pomegranate in half and using the back of a wooden spoon, knock each half into a bowl to release the fruit and collect any juices. Set aside.

Hold back some of the pomegranate fruit to serve as a garnish with the pudding.

Mix the pomegranate juice and chia seeds together in a bowl and whisk fairly briskly with a fork.

Leave the seeds to stand and soak for about 15-20 minutes, stirring regularly in that time so that the seeds don't sink to the bottom of the bowl.

Fold in most of the pomegranate as well as the juice that was collected. Refrigerate for a few hours before serving.

Serve with yoghurt and the reserved pomegranate.

NOTE: THIS IS MY FAVOURITE CHIA PUDDING AS I FIND IT LIGHT AND VERY REFRESHING, PLUS I LOVE THE DEEP RED COLOUR, ESPECIALLY AGAINST THE BLACK CHIA SEEDS. THIS PUDDING IS GREAT AS A DESSERT BUT ALSO DELICIOUS FOR BREAKFAST, DOLLOPED OVER A BOWL OF YOGHURT.

VANILLA AND CINNAMON PUDDING IN A JAR

SERVES 1–2

1 cup almond milk or milk of
   your choice
3 tablespoons chia seeds
1–2 tablespoons honey
1 teaspoon vanilla bean paste
   or vanilla extract
1/4 – 1/2 teaspoon ground
   cinnamon

Place all the ingredients into a glass jar with a tight-fitting lid and mix together. Make sure you stir the bottom of the jar to ensure the honey dissolves and all the ingredients have combined.

Cover the jar with the lid and shake vigorously for 1–2 minutes. Place in the refrigerator for about 1 hour before using. The pudding improves the longer it is in the fridge and has time to absorb all the flavours.

Prepare it the night before and leave in the fridge until the morning. If you think the pudding is too thick just mix in a little extra milk.

The pudding will keep in the fridge for over a week. This is lovely for breakfast and a convenient breakfast on the go, as the jar makes it easy to transport.

NOTE: THIS IS THE BASIC RECIPE FOR A QUICK TO MAKE, NO FUSS, NO GADGET PUDDING. YOU CAN VARY YOUR FLAVOURINGS AND SWEETNESS TO SUIT YOUR INDIVIDUAL TASTE.
IF YOU WOULD PREFER A SMOOTHER PUDDING, YOU CAN USE A BLENDER AND BLITZ EVERYTHING BEFORE PLACING IN THE REFRIGERATOR.
WHEN THIS PUDDING IS MADE WITH WHOLE MILK, IT REMINDS ME OF THE GREEK RICE PUDDING 'RIZOGALO'.

SPICED POTATO WEDGES

Preheat the oven to 400°F/200°C and line a large baking tray with non-stick baking paper.

After cutting, dry again with paper towels; the potatoes should be as dry as possible before coating with the other ingredients.

Pour the coconut oil over the potatoes and rub in to coat completely and thoroughly.

Mix together the chia seeds, cumin, paprika, curry, turmeric, chilli and garlic salt. Sprinkle the spice mixture over the potatoes and completely coat them all over.

Spread the potatoes onto the prepared tray in a single layer and bake in the oven for 30–40 minutes until golden, crisp and tender.

Taste and season with extra sea salt if necessary.

Serve with sour cream and sweet chilli sauce.

2 lb 4 oz/1 kg potatoes
2 tablespoons organic raw coconut oil or extra virgin olive oil
2 tablespoons chia seeds
1 tablespoon cumin seeds
1 teaspoon ground paprika
1/2 teaspoon curry powder
1/2 teaspoon ground turmeric
1/2 teaspoon dried chilli flakes
1 teaspoon garlic salt
low-fat sour cream, for serving
sweet chilli sauce, for serving

NOTE: THE CHIA SEEDS ADD A LOVELY CRUNCH TO THESE HEALTHY HOMEMADE POTATO WEDGES. KEEP THE SPICE MIX ON HAND BY MIXING THE CHIA AND CUMIN SEEDS WITH THE PAPRIKA, CURRY POWDER, TURMERIC, CHILLI FLAKES AND SALT TOGETHER AND STORING IN A JAR WITH A TIGHT-FITTING LID.

SEAWEED

Seaweed is super nutritious, being one of the most nutritionally dense plants and offering the broadest range of minerals. Seaweeds contain almost all the nutrients available in the ocean.

High in nutrients and low in calories, the many varieties of seaweed are all excellent sources of B vitamins, vitamins A, C, E, K, folate, calcium, iron, magnesium, iodine, selenium, riboflavin and pantothenic acid.

Seaweed also contains B12, a vitamin not usually found in vegetables, and also contains the plant compound lignan, which has cancer-protecting properties.

Lignan is known to inhibit blood cell growth, which is the process by which fast-growing tumours not only survive but also spread to form secondary tumours in other parts of the body.

Seaweed is packed with antioxidants and aids in detoxification, increases metabolism, helps with weight control, can prevent osteoporosis, keeps hair and skin healthy, and helps relieve stress.

It is also believed that seaweed can be beneficial for and improve the health of your heart. It can reduce cholesterol levels in the blood, help reduce high blood pressure and help prevent hardening of the arteries (arteriosclerosis).

Seaweed also has 14 times more calcium than milk. It is high in protein and low in fat with no carbohydrates. Seaweed is also thought to be very effective in combating bacterial and viral infections.

It is also said that the nutrients found in seaweed can be up to 60 times more potent than land vegetables. The Japanese and Korean cultures have known for centuries just how powerful the health benefits of sea vegetation actually is and that it is a rich source of iodine. Iodine is essential for a healthy thyroid and neurological function.

Varieties

There are many different types of seaweeds, all with different flavours and textures. Some of them can be quite chewy, others can be soft, some are strong tasting and some are mild-tasting, depending on how they are prepared.

Wakame—long ribbon-like leaves that can have a sweet-salty taste.

Nori—paper-thin sheets with a very mild sea taste. The most common and probably best known, used around sushi rolls.

Arame—very long and thin strands more on the sweet side.

Kelp—also known as brown algae, has thick leaves.

Dulse—red-purple rubbery leaves.

It should also be remembered that some but not all varieties of seaweed are high in sodium.

How to buy and prepare seaweed

I have only ever been able to buy dehydrated seaweed, which I can find at most of the Asian grocery shops. They are very inexpensive and the advantage of buying them dry is that you can always have a packet or two of your favourite seaweed on hand. Which type of seaweed you use is really of personal preference. I have specified some by name in some of the recipes but you can use whichever one appeals most.

Rehydrate seaweed by soaking it in cold water for about 5 minutes, then drain well. I find it is easier to cut seaweed into smaller pieces before soaking. In some recipes, such as soup, the seaweed can be added straight into the soup and rehydrated while the soup cooks, depending on which seaweed you use and the length of the cooking time. Some seaweed is quite deceptive as it looks very small and thin, but once you rehydrate, you find that it is in quite large pieces.

Also, dried seaweed is very light and sometimes tricky to weigh properly. As a general rule 3 oz/10 g of dried seaweed is usually about a cupful, once it has been broken into small pieces. Remember, though, that as small as the amount may seem in the dried state, once it is rehydrated the volume increases quite a bit.

Precaution

There is a general concern about where seaweed is harvested from and the levels of toxins present in the seaweed when consumed. The main concern is the presence arsenic or toxic metals. If the water the seaweed comes from is contaminated then it would be safe to say that the seaweed will be as well. Caution should be exercised when buying seaweed and ensuring that the seaweed you purchase comes from a reputable source.

It should also be noted that seaweed comes with certain components that may interfere with blood thinning medications. If you are taking such medications it is advisable to watch your intake of seaweed and not to be excessive with the amount consumed, and consult your physician for their advice before you start eating it.

CHICKEN, SHIITAKE MUSHROOM AND SEAWEED SOUP

SERVES 6

8 cups chicken stock
1 stalk lemongrass, bruised
2 star anise
1 knob fresh ginger, sliced
1 large clove garlic, peeled and
   lightly smashed
9 oz/250 g chicken thigh
   fillets, very thinly sliced
⅔ oz/20 g dried seaweed, cut
   into small pieces
½ oz/15 g sliced dried shiitake
   mushrooms
1 red chilli, sliced
1 tablespoon fish sauce
2 tablespoons tamari soy sauce
fresh bean sprouts, for garnish
4-6 scallions/spring onions,
   thinly sliced, for garnish
sliced red chilli, for garnish

Bring the stock to the boil in a large saucepan with the lemongrass, star anise, ginger and garlic.

Once the stock is boiling, add the chicken, seaweed, mushrooms, chilli, fish sauce and soy sauce.

Reduce the heat, cover and simmer on low heat for 15 minutes until the chicken is cooked and the seaweed and mushrooms are soft.

Remove the lemongrass and star anise and serve garnished with some bean sprouts, sliced scallions and chillies.

NOTE: YOU CAN LEAVE OUT THE CHICKEN FOR A VEGETARIAN OPTION OR REPLACE IT WITH ANOTHER TYPE OF MEAT OR SEAFOOD.

SHRIMP AND SEAWEED PANCAKES WITH BONITO FLAKES

MAKES 4 PANCAKES

1-2 teaspoons oil

6-8 scallions/spring onions, sliced

1 red chilli

4 extra large eggs

1½ cups self-raising flour

½ teaspoon sea salt

2 cups water

2 teaspoons dashi powder

1 tablespoon soy sauce

⅓ oz/10 g thinly sliced dried roasted nori seaweed

5 oz/150 g cooked and peeled shrimp/prawns

bonito flakes, for garnish

3 scallions/spring onions, thinly sliced (extra), for garnish

sliced red chilli (extra), for garnish

DRESSING

4 tablespoons light soy sauce

2 tablespoons rice vinegar or white wine vinegar

1 teaspoon sesame oil

finely sliced red chillies

Heat the oil in a frying pan and cook the scallions and chilli until soft. Remove from the heat and set aside.

Whisk together the eggs, flour, salt, water, dashi powder and soy sauce until you have a smooth batter.

Stir in the seaweed and leave to stand for about 5 minutes to soften the seaweed, then mix in the shrimp, extra scallions and chillies.

Heat a little oil in a small non-stick frying pan and, when hot, add a ladleful of the mixture and swirl the pan around so as to evenly distribute the batter.

Cook on low-medium heat until the pancake is almost set and the bottom is browned.

Turn over with a spatula and cook for further 2-3 minutes until set.

Serve garnished with bonito flakes, scallions and chillies and a drizzle of the dressing.

To make the dressing, mix all the ingredients together.

NOTE: YOU CAN SUBSTITUTE THE SHRIMP/PRAWNS WITH COOKED CHICKEN OR BACON OR LEAVE OUT ALTOGETHER. DASHI POWDER IS POWDERED STOCK AND AVAILABLE AT SOME SUPERMARKETS AND MOST ASIAN GROCERY STORES.

SEAWEED TEMPURA

Soak the seaweed in cold water for 5 minutes until rehydrated.

In the meantime, sift the flours and baking powder into a bowl, then stir in the sesame seeds, chilli flakes and salt.

Whisk in the soda water until you get a thickish but loose batter and set aside.

Drain the seaweed really well then cut or tear it into different-sized pieces and pat dry with kitchen paper until it is as dry as possible.

Dip the seaweed into the batter and coat well.

Heat about 5 cm/2 in of oil in a deep-frying pan on medium-high heat until hot.

Gently and carefully place the battered seaweed into the hot oil and fry until just golden on both sides. Do this in batches and avoid over-crowding the pan so that they cook evenly.

Remove from the hot oil with a slotted spoon and place on kitchen paper to drain away any excess oil.

Serve immediately with a light sprinkling of salt and the dipping sauce.

To make the dipping sauce, mix together the soy sauce and the sliced red chillies.

⅔ oz/20 g dried wakame seaweed
½ cup all-purpose/plain flour
1 tablespoon cornstarch/ cornflour
½ teaspoon baking powder
2 tablespoons white sesame seeds
chilli flakes, to taste
salt, to taste
¾ cup icy cold soda water
oil, for frying
salt, extra, for serving

DIPPING SAUCE
soy sauce
thinly sliced red chillies

NOTE: THESE ARE VERY QUICK AND EASY TO PREPARE AS THEY USE INGREDIENTS THAT ARE ON HAND IN MOST PANTRIES. THE AMOUNT OF SEAWEED THAT YOU WILL NEED MAY VARY DEPENDING ON WHAT SIZE THE SEAWEED IS CUT INTO.

CITRUS AND CHILLI SALAD

SERVES 4–6

⅔ oz/20 g dried wakame
   seaweed
juice 1 large orange, strained
juice 1 grapefruit, strained
1 tablespoon sesame seeds
1-2 long red chillies, sliced
2 teaspoons toasted sesame oil
2 teaspoons rice vinegar
2 teaspoons sweet chilli sauce
salt (optional)

Cut the seaweed into small pieces and place into a bowl with the orange and grapefruit juice. Leave to soak for 15-20 minutes until the seaweed rehydrates.

In the meantime, place the sesame seeds into a small non-stick frying pan over medium heat and toast until golden. Keep an eye on them and toss the pan regularly as they can burn very easily

When the seaweed is rehydrated and has absorbed most, if not all of the juice, add the sliced chillies, with or without the seeds, the sesame oil, rice vinegar and sweet chilli sauce, and salt to taste.

Mix well then stir through the sesame seeds. This salad is best if it can be set aside for about 1 hour so that all the flavours can be absorbed and combine together.

NOTE: YOU CAN REPLACE THE WAKAME SEAWEED WITH OTHER TYPES OF SEAWEED, BUT USE A HARDY SEAWEED THAT CAN WITHSTAND THE CITRUS JUICE AND NOT A THIN ONE, LIKE NORI SEAWEED.

MISO SOUP

SERVES 4

Place the water and dashi powder into a saucepan and bring to the boil.

Add the seaweed and mushrooms and bring back to the boil, reduce the heat to a low simmer, cover and cook for about 10 minutes until the seaweed and mushrooms are soft.

Slowly stir in the miso paste and keep stirring until the paste dissolves, then bring back to the boil.

Add the scallions simmer on low heat for 1-2 minutes. Serve immediately.

5 cups water
⅓ oz/10 g (2 teaspoons) dashi powder
⅓ oz/10 g dried seaweed, broken into small pieces
½ oz/15 g sliced dried shiitake mushrooms
¼ cup white miso paste
4 thin scallions/spring onions, sliced diagonally

NOTE: THIS IS A VERY QUICK AND TASTY SOUP TO MAKE; I HAVE PURPOSELY USED DRIED MUSHROOMS SO THAT THIS SOUP CAN BE PREPARED AT ANY TIME USING INGREDIENTS AVAILABLE IN THE KITCHEN PANTRY. MISO PASTE WILL KEEP IN THE REFRIGERATOR FOR SOME TIME ONCE OPENED, PROVIDED IT IS USED BEFORE THE BEST BY DATE.

YOU CAN USE FRESH SHIITAKE MUSHROOMS OR YOU CAN EVEN REPLACE THE MUSHROOM WITH TOFU.

SUSHI BALLS

Rinse the rice under cold running water, drain and place into a saucepan with the water. Bring to the boil, reduce heat, cover and simmer for about 12–15 minutes until all the water is absorbed.

In the meantime, dissolve the sugar in the vinegar and set aside.

Remove the rice from the heat, stir in the seaweed flakes (you can add as much or as little as you like), taste and season with a little salt if you think it's necessary, and leave to stand, covered, for about 5 minutes.

Place the rice into a non-metallic bowl and stir in the vinegar mixture, then gently mix to thoroughly combine. Cool the rice until it is cool enough to handle.

Take teaspoonfuls of the rice and, using wet hands, roll it into balls of whatever size you prefer. I find the size of a small walnut to be good. Serve with wasabi paste.

1 cup sushi rice
1½ cups water
1 tablespoon sugar
2 tablespoons rice wine vinegar
1–1½ cups seasoned seaweed flakes (available from health food stores)
salt, to taste
wasabi paste, for serving

NOTE: CAN BE MADE IN ADVANCE AND STORED IN THE FRIDGE UP TO A DAY AHEAD. YOU CAN LEAVE THESE SUSHI BALLS AS THEY ARE, OR YOU CAN ADD A FILLING, SUCH AS CUBES OF CUCUMBER, CARROT OR AVOCADO: PIECES OF SEAFOOD, SUCH AS SALMON, TUNA, CRAB OR SHRIMPS/PRAWNS; OR COOKED CHICKEN. TAKE A SPOONFUL OF RICE AND FLATTEN IT IN THE PALM OF YOUR HAND. PLACE A SMALL AMOUNT OF THE FILLING OF YOUR CHOICE, THEN ROLL INTO A BALL TO ENCLOSE THE FILLING. SUSHI BALLS WITH FILLING SHOULD BE CONSUMED WITHIN A FEW HOURS.

SUSHI WITH AMARANTH

MAKES 4—6 LARGE SUSHI ROLLS

2 teaspoons sugar

3 tablespoons rice wine vinegar

1 cup sushi rice

⅓ cup amaranth grain

2¼ cups water

4-6 nori sheets

wasabi paste

fillings: fresh salmon, tuna, avocado, strips of cucumber, strips of carrot, crab, chicken, shrimp/prawns, bell pepper/capsicum, scallions/spring onions

Dissolve the sugar in the vinegar and set aside.

Rinse and drain the rice and place in a saucepan with the amaranth and water, stir well, bring to the boil, then reduce the heat, cover and simmer for 15-20 minutes until all the water is absorbed.

Remove from the heat, transfer to a non-metallic bowl then stir in the vinegar mix and cool completely.

Place the nori sheet, shiny side down, onto the bamboo rolling mat.

Divide the rice and amaranth mixture into four or six depending on how much rice mixture you prefer, and, using wet finger tips, spread evenly over the nori sheet, leaving a 1 in/2 cm border at the bottom end away from you.

Dab a small amount of wasabi in a straight line at the edge closest to you. Place the fillings of your choice on top of the wasabi in a neat line.

Lift the bamboo mat at the closest edge to you and begin to slowly and tightly roll the nori sheet, at the same time separating the bamboo mat away from the rolled part of the nori sheet.

Lightly wet the end of the sheet and gently press to join the edge together.

Using a wet serrated knife, slice the sushi in half or in 5-6 pieces.

NOTE: YOU WILL NEED A BAMBOO ROLLING MAT FOR THIS RECIPE.

BY ADDING AMARANTH TO THE RICE YOU CAN ADD A DIFFERENT TEXTURE AS WELL AS MAKING THESE ROLLS EVEN HEALTHIER.

SUSHI ROLLS ARE TRADITIONALLY SERVED WITH PICKLED GINGER AND SOY SAUCE FOR DIPPING.

STIR-FRIED SEAWEED

SERVES 4–6

1¾ oz/50 g dried wakame seaweed
1 teaspoon miso paste
1 cup water
1-2 tablespoons oil
4 cloves garlic, peeled and sliced
2 long red chillies, sliced
1 large thumb-sized knob of ginger, sliced
2 tablespoons light soy sauce
4 scallions/spring onions, sliced diagonally
½ -1 teaspoon sesame oil
1 tablespoon sesame seeds (optional)

Place the seaweed into a bowl of cold water and leave to soak and rehydrate for 10 minutes. Drain well to remove all the excess water.

Dissolve the miso paste in the water and set aside (you can use the water from the seaweed if you like).

Heat oil in a large frying pan or wok until hot; add the garlic, chilli and ginger stir-fry 1-2 minutes until fragrant and they start to take on some colour but without burning.

Add the seaweed and stir-fry until incorporated with the garlic, chilli and ginger and cook for 2-3 minutes tossing constantly.

Add the soy sauce and as much of the miso mixture as you feel necessary to create a sauce and continue cooking for another 2-3 minutes, stirring constantly.

Toss in the shallots and sprinkle in the sesame oil and cook for another 1-2 minutes

Serve with hot steaming rice.

NOTE: YOU CAN ADD MEAT TO THIS DISH BY STIR-FRYING SOME THIN STRIPS OF BEEF, PORK OR CHICKEN IN A LITTLE OIL AND GARLIC UNTIL COOKED. REMOVE FROM THE PAN AND SET ASIDE THEN COOK SEAWEED AS ABOVE. WHEN SEAWEED IS READY TOSS THROUGH THE COOKED MEAT AND ANY JUICES THAT MAY HAVE ACCUMULATED.

SEAWEED SOUP WITH MINCED BEEF

Cut the seaweed into small strips and soak the in lukewarm water for about 5 minutes until soft. Drain and rinse, then squeeze out any excess water.

Heat the oils in a large saucepan until hot, add the mince and cook for 2-3 minutes.

Slice the chillies either with or without the seeds, and add to the mince with the seaweed, scallions, garlic and soy sauce, and cook for about 2 minutes.

Pour in the stock, bring to the boil, reduce the heat, cover and simmer for 20-30 minutes.

Season with salt and pepper if you think necessary and serve with freshly squeezed lemon or lime juice and sliced chillies.

1 oz/30 g dried wakame seaweed
1 tablespoon oil
1 teaspoon sesame oil
9 oz/250 g minced beef or pork
2 long red chillies
4 scallions/spring onions, sliced
2 cloves garlic, finely chopped
2 tablespoons light soy sauce
8 cups hot chicken stock
salt and freshly cracked black pepper (optional)
lemon or lime juice, for serving
extra red chillies, for garnish

NOTE: I LIKE TO USE CHICKEN STOCK IN THIS SOUP AS I THINK IT MAKES A LIGHTER SOUP, ESPECIALLY IF YOU ARE USING PORK. YOU CAN, HOWEVER, USE EITHER DASHI STOCK OR A BEEF OR VEGETABLE STOCK. AND YOU CAN ALSO SUBSTITUTE VERY FINE STRIPS OF CHICKEN OR CHICKEN MINCE FOR THE BEEF OR PORK MINCE.

SEAWEED SALAD

SERVES 4–6

⅔ oz/20 g shredded, dried seaweed
1 Lebanese cucumber, cut into thin strips
1 medium carrot, cut into thin strips
1 red bell pepper/capsicum, cut into thin strips
1 red onion, halved and thinly sliced
1 teaspoon finely grated fresh ginger
1 tablespoon white wine vinegar or rice wine vinegar
1-2 tablespoons extra virgin olive oil
splash of sesame oil
sesame seeds, toasted, for serving

Cut the seaweed into small pieces, place in a bowl of cold water and leave to rehydrate for 5 minutes. Drain well and leave to stand in a colander to drain off any excess water while you prepare the remaining ingredients.

Cut the cucumber, carrot and bell pepper into very thin strips about 1½ in/4 cm in length.

Place into a bowl with the onion, ginger, seaweed, vinegar and oils. Toss well so that all the ingredients are thoroughly mixed together.

Allow salad to stand for about ½–1 hour for all the flavours to combine.

Transfer onto a serving platter and sprinkle with toasted sesame seeds before serving.

NOTE: DRIED SEAWEED CAN BE QUITE DECEPTIVE, WHEN DRY THE PIECES CAN LOOK QUITE THIN AND SMALL IN SIZE BUT ONCE REHYDRATED THE PIECES WILL EXPAND TO BE MUCH LARGER.

RAW
CACAO

Raw cacao is the unprocessed, raw form of chocolate that grows in seeds on small trees called *Theobroma cacao*, which is derived from the Greek 'theos' and 'broma', meaning 'food of the gods'. These trees are native to Mexico, Central and South America. Raw cacao is NOT the same as cocoa powder. Raw cacao is made by processing unroasted cocoa beans. Cocoa powder is raw cacao that has been roasted at high temperatures, thereby reducing the healthy living enzymes found in raw cacao.

Raw cacao is a rich source of flavonoids. These natural antioxidants are found in plants, and raw cacao is considered a superfood because it contains more flavonoids than any other food. In fact, it contains more antioxidants than green tea, black tea, red wine and even blueberries.

Are you eating dark chocolate because you think it's healthier than milk chocolate? Most of the dark chocolate available is very highly processed by roasting and combining with other ingredients, such as sugar and some form of fat. As a result, it loses valuable nutrients and the strength of the antioxidants is reduced.

On the other hand, raw cacao beans, once removed from their pods, are put through a natural fermentation process then dried over a week or so, leaving all their important vitamins and minerals intact.

Not that most people need an excuse for eating some form of chocolate but here are some reasons that are particularly beneficial to us when eating chocolate in the 'raw cacao' form just in case you need convincing.

Apart from containing more flavonoids than any other food. There are also some important vitamins and minerals present, such as vitamins B1, B2, B3, B5, B9, E, magnesium, manganese, iron, copper, zinc, sulphur and potassium.

Raw cacao also contains oleic acid, a monounsaturated fat, as well as protein and fibre. The amount of magnesium found in raw cacao is higher than in any other food and magnesium is regarded as the most significant mineral in relaxing muscles and relieving stress. It is also important in building strong teeth and bones.

The antioxidants and other elements found in raw cacao can promote healthy cardiovascular function by lowering blood pressure, improving blood flow, reducing clogging of the arteries and lowering cholesterol.

This high level of antioxidants can also help reduce the build-up of free radicals within the body which could cause cancer.

Raw cacao can also aid our digestive system by stimulating the digestive enzymes in our bodies.

Purchasing raw cacao

When buying raw cacao you should look for labels that say 'raw cacao' or 'cacao beans that are not roasted' and it is also a good idea to purchase organic raw cacao.

Raw cacao comes in powder form or cacao nibs and even cacao butter. I have mainly used the powdered cacao for the recipes in this book. It should be noted that raw cacao is quite bitter, especially in the form of the nibs as they are more concentrated bits of cacao and are also quite hard to bite on. Chopping them into smaller pieces can be a good idea for certain uses. The bitterness comes from the fact that they are still in the raw state before any roasting or mixing with any sugars or fat takes place.

The nibs can be used as toppings sprinkled over ice cream or muffins or in any recipe where you need to use pieces of chocolate, like chocolate chips. I like to sprinkle them over frosting on cakes

Usually all forms of raw cacao are available from health food stores or online.

CACAO AND QUINOA CHOCOLATE CHIP COOKIES

MAKES 15—18 COOKIES

1½ cups quinoa flour
1 teaspoon baking powder
½ teaspoon baking soda/
  bicarbonate of soda
3 tablespoons pure raw
  cacao powder
8 oz/250 g white chocolate
  chips
4 oz/125 g butter, at room
  temperature
¾ cup brown sugar, loosely
  packed
2 teaspoons vanilla extract
2 extra large eggs
2 tablespoons low-fat milk

Preheat the oven to 180°C /350°F and grease and line 2 baking trays with non-stick baking paper.

Sift together the flour, baking powder, baking soda and cacao then stir in the chocolate chips and set aside.

Cream the butter and brown sugar together until light and creamy.

Beat in the vanilla and eggs, then fold in the flour mixture and the milk and mix until well combined. Mixture will be soft and sticky.

Place teaspoonfuls of cookie dough the size of a large walnut on to baking tray.

Bake for about 11-12 minutes. Biscuits should not be overcooked and still be a little soft when taken out of the oven.

Cool biscuits completely in the tray before removing them and storing in an airtight container.

NOTE: QUINOA FLOUR CAN BE REPLACED WITH REGULAR WHEATEN FLOUR. I WOULD LIKE TO THANK MY GORGEOUS GRANDCHILDREN MADISON AND KOBE FOR HELPING MAKE THESE COOKIES FOR THE PHOTOS—THEN, OF COURSE, VERY QUICKLY MAKING THEM DISAPPEAR!

CACAO AND ALMOND DRINK

SERVES 2

2 cups icy cold almond milk
2 level tablespoons pure raw
   cacao powder
1 teaspoon vanilla extract
1-2 teaspoons organic raw
   coconut oil
1 tablespoon maple syrup or
   natural sweetener of choice
pinch of cinnamon
ice cubes

Place all ingredients into a blender and blend on high speed for about 20 seconds until you have a drink that has a thick and smooth consistency.

   The amount of sweetener added is of personal preference. Normally I find almond milk to be sweet enough; however, the raw cacao is quite bitter and most people may want some amount of sweetener added.

NOTE: YOU CAN SUBSTITUTE ALMOND MILK WITH WHICHEVER OTHER MILK IS YOUR FAVOURITE.

CASHEW, CRANBERRY AND COCONUT POWER BALLS

MAKES 25–30

Soak the dates in hot water for 5 minutes to soften, then drain well.

Place the cashews in a food processor and process until they are chopped into very small pieces.

Add the dates and all of the other ingredients except for the orange juice and extra coconut and process until all the fruit and nuts are finely chopped.

Add as much orange juice as is needed and continue processing until you have a fine and moist paste, but not too wet.

Lightly wet your hands and roll the mixture into balls the size of a small walnut or whatever size you prefer, then roll in the extra coconut.

Refrigerate until they become firm, then store in a covered container.

5 oz/150 g pitted Medjool dates
5 oz/150 g raw cashews
4 oz/125 g golden raisins/ sultanas
3 oz/90 g dried cranberries
2 tablespoons organic raw coconut oil
1 cup desiccated coconut
4 tablespoons pure raw cacao powder
1 teaspoon vanilla bean paste
2-3 tablespoons orange juice
desiccated coconut (extra), for finishing

NOTE: CHECK FOR SWEETNESS BEFORE YOU ROLL THESE AS THERE HAS BEEN NO SWEETENER ADDED TO THIS MIXTURE. IF YOU DO NOT FIND THEM SWEET ENOUGH ADD SOME HONEY OR AGAVE SYRUP.

CHILLI BEEF

Heat the oil in a large saucepan and sauté the onion until golden. Add the meat and continue cooking until browned all over.

Stir in the garlic and bell peppers and cook for 1-2 minutes, then add the oregano, cumin, paprika and chilli, and cook until fragrant.

Stir in the tomatoes, sugar, cacao, water and season with salt. Bring to the boil, reduce the heat, cover and simmer on low heat for about 25-30 minutes until the meat is tender.

Stir in the red kidney beans and continue cooking on low heat until the beans are heated through.

Serve with fresh chopped cilantro, a dollop of yoghurt and slices of avocado.

2 tablespoons olive oil
1 large onion, finely chopped
1 lb/500 g rump steak,
  cut into strips
3 cloves garlic, chopped
2 red bell peppers/capsicums,
  diced
1½ teaspoons ground oregano
2 heaped teaspoons ground
  cumin
1 teaspoon ground paprika
1-2 teaspoons dried chilli flakes
2 x 14 oz/400 g cans diced
  tomatoes
1 teaspoon sugar
1-2 tablespoons pure raw
  cacao powder
1 cup water
salt, to taste
2 x 14 oz/400 g cans red
  kidney beans, drained and
  rinsed
fresh chopped cilantro/
  coriander, for serving
Greek yoghurt, for serving
sliced avocado, for serving

NOTE: HOW MUCH CACAO YOU USE IS TOTALLY UP TO YOU, THE MORE YOU USE THE RICHER, THICKER AND DARKER THE CHILLI WILL BE, WITH A SLIGHT BITTERNESS TO IT—THAT'S WHY THE ADDITION OF A LITTLE SUGAR. THE LESS SUGAR YOU USE THE MORE SUBTLE THE FLAVOUR. THE COOKING TIME WILL ALSO DEPEND ON THE CUT OF BEEF THAT YOU USE.

SUPER BROWNIES

Preheat the oven to 350°F/180°C and lightly grease and line a 9½ in/24 cm square non-stick baking tin.

Sift the cacao into a bowl and stir in the coffee and sugar.

Whisk together the butter, eggs and vanilla, then slowly, mix in the cacao and sugar mixture.

Sift the flour with the baking powder and salt, add to the cacao mixture and mix until thoroughly combined.

Fold in the walnuts and chocolate chips and pour into the prepared tin. Give the tin a good tap on your kitchen counter before placing in the oven. Bake for about 25 minutes.

Cool in the tin before turning out, cutting and dusting with a little raw cacao powder before serving.

¾ cup raw cacao
1 teaspoon instant coffee
1 cup granulated sugar
6 oz/180 g butter, melted
4 extra large eggs
2 teaspoons vanilla extract
¾ cups quinoa flour
2 teaspoons baking powder
pinch of salt
1 cup chopped walnuts
1 cup cacao nibs or chocolate chips
raw cacao, for dusting

NOTE: THESE BROWNIES HAVE ALWAYS BEEN SUCH A HUGE HIT WITH EVERYONE WHO HAS EVER TRIED THEM. THEY ARE TRULY DELICIOUS AND WILL DISAPPEAR VERY QUICKLY. STORE IN AN AIRTIGHT CONTAINER—THEY ARE JUST AS DELICIOUS STORED IN THE REFRIGERATOR AND EATEN COLD.

CHICKEN WITH CACAO MOLE SAUCE

SERVES 4

2 tablespoons olive oil
8 chicken thigh cutlets
1 large red onion, roughly
  chopped
4 cloves garlic, roughly
  chopped
sesame seeds, toasted, for
  serving

MOLE SAUCE
2 tablespoons pure raw cacao
  powder
2 long red chillies, roughly
  chopped
2 long green chillies, roughly
  chopped
½ –1 teaspoon dried chilli flakes
1 x 14 oz/400 g can tomatoes,
  undrained
½ cup golden raisins/sultanas
1 corn tortilla, cut into pieces
½ teaspoon ground cinnamon
1 teaspoon ground cumin
½ teaspoon fennel seeds
1 star anise
¼ teaspoon ground cloves
salt
1 cup chicken stock

Heat the oil in a large saucepan and brown the chicken all over in two batches. Remove from the pan and set aside. Leave about 2 tablespoons of oil in the saucepan and discard the rest.

Add the onion and garlic to the pan and sauté until soft and golden.

Place the garlic and onion mixture in a food processor with all the sauce ingredients and process until you have a smooth paste.

Return the chicken to the saucepan with the sauce, bring to the boil, reduce the heat, cover and simmer for about 45 minutes until the chicken is cooked.

Dry toast the sesame seeds in a small non-stick frying pan and sprinkle over the chicken when serving.

Serve the chicken with plain boiled or steamed rice.

NOTE: CHICKEN CUTLETS, ALSO KNOWN AS CHICKEN CHOPS, ARE THE THIGH WITH THE RIB PART OF THE BONE REMOVED AND JUST THE THICKISH THIGH BONE LEFT IN THEM. I FIND THEM IDEAL FOR THIS DISH. HOW MANY CHILLIES YOU USE IN THIS DISH IS TOTALLY UP TO YOU AND WILL DEPEND ON HOW SPICY YOU LIKE YOUR FOOD.

HOT CHOCOLATE

Place all the ingredients into a blender or food processor and blend on high speed for about 20 seconds until you have a smooth consistency.

Pour into a medium saucepan and gently heat until hot. Serve with or without marshmallows.

4 level tablespoons pure raw cacao powder
3-4 tablespoons sugar or sweetener of choice
1 teaspoon vanilla bean paste
4 cups milk
marshmallows, for serving (optional)

NOTE: SOMETIMES THERE IS NOTHING BETTER THAN A CUP OF HOT CHOCOLATE, ESPECIALLY ON THOSE COLD WINTERY DAYS. IT HAS BEEN KNOWN TO INSTIL A FEELING OF WELLBEING. IF YOU HAVE EVER FELT GUILTY ABOUT DOING SO, MAKE THIS GUILT-FREE VERSION USING RAW CACAO.

DATE, FIG AND MINT ENERGY BALLS

MAKES 25

4 oz/125 g pitted Medjool
   dates
5 oz/150 g dried figs
4 oz/125 g almonds, with the
   skin on
4 tablespoons pure raw cacao
   powder
2 tablespoons organic raw
   coconut oil
½ teaspoon pure mint extract
   (or to taste)
1-2 tablespoons reserved liquid
sifted cacao powder (extra),
   for dusting
raw cacao nibs (optional), for
   coating

Soak the dates and figs in hot water for 5 minutes to soften, then drain well and reserve the liquid.

Place almonds into a food processor and process until they are finely chopped.

Add the dates, figs, cacao powder, coconut oil, mint extract and reserved liquid and continue processing until the mixture turns into a fine moist paste. (It is a good idea to start by using half the quantity of liquid specified then adding the rest if need be.)

Lightly wet your hands and roll the mixture into balls about the size of a small walnut or whatever size you prefer, then lightly roll each ball in the sifted cacao powder.

If you wish, crush the cacao nibs until you have very small pieces then lightly roll the cacao-covered balls into the cacao nibs. Keep in mind that both the cacao powder and the cacao nibs can be quite bitter on their own.

NOTE: CHECK FOR SWEETNESS BEFORE YOU ROLL THESE AS NO SWEETENER HAS BEEN ADDED TO THIS MIXTURE. IF NOT SWEET ENOUGH FOR YOU, ADD A LITTLE HONEY OR AGAVE SYRUP. I FIND THE COMBINATION OF THE DRIED DATES AND FIGS TO BE QUITE SWEET AND WELCOME THE SLIGHT BITTERNESS OF THE RAW CACAO AS A COATING.

SIENNA CAKE

SERVES 8–10

4 oz/125 g blanched almonds
4 oz/125 g hazelnuts
2 oz/60 g dried apricots
2 oz/60 g glacé pineapple
2 oz/60 g glacé cherries
2 oz/60 g mixed peel
½ cup all-purpose/plain flour
1 teaspoon ground cinnamon
¼ – ½ teaspoon ground
   nutmeg
3 level tablespoons pure raw
   cacao powder
⅔ cup honey
½ cup light brown sugar
1 oz/30 g butter
1 teaspoon vanilla bean paste
   or extract
confectioner's/icing sugar, for
   dusting

Preheat the oven to 325°F/160°C and grease and line an 8 in/20 cm round cake tin with non-stick baking paper.

Roughly chop the almonds, hazelnuts, apricots, pineapple and cherries. Place in a bowl and mix in the mixed peel.

Sift together the flour, cinnamon, nutmeg and raw cacao. Add this mixture to the fruit and gently mix until combined.

Place the honey, sugar and butter into a small saucepan and gently simmer until the sugar melts and the mixture bubbles.

Remove from the heat, stir in the vanilla and mix well into the fruit mixture. You have to mix the honey mixture in fairly quickly as it starts to set as soon as it is taken off the heat.

Spread the fruit mixture into the prepared cake tin. Use the back of a metal spoon, dipped in hot water, to spread it out. Bake for 35 minutes.

Cool completely in tin then when cooled, remove from tin and wrap in foil.

Leave to stand overnight before dusting liberally with sifted icing sugar and slicing into thin wedges.

NOTE: THIS IS A VERY RICH TRADITIONAL ITALIAN CAKE AND IS USUALLY SERVED CUT INTO THIN SLICES.

RAW CACAO, CHIA AND CINNAMON BLISS BALLS

MAKES 20—24

5 oz/150 g Medjool dates, pitted
5 oz/150 g raw almonds or cashews
⅓ cup pure raw cacao powder
1½ teaspoons ground cinnamon
3 tablespoons melted organic raw coconut oil
1 tablespoon chia seeds
1½ teaspoons vanilla paste
1 tablespoon honey or agave syrup
extra raw cacao powder, for coating (optional)

Soak the dates in hot water for 5 minutes to soften, then drain well.

In the meantime, place the almonds or cashews into a food processor and process until finely chopped.

Add the dates, cacao powder, cinnamon, coconut oil, chia seeds, vanilla and honey to the food processor and process until the mixture comes together and you have a paste.

Wet the palms of your hands with cold water and roll mixture into walnut-sized balls or another size that suits, and then lightly coat with the extra cacao powder, or leave as is.

Refrigerate for at least 1-2 hours before serving.

These can be stored in the refrigerator in a container with a lid.

NOTE: WHEN COATING THESE, KEEP IN MIND THAT RAW CACAO POWDER IS QUITE BITTER SO A LIGHT COATING IS BEST. BEFORE ROLLING INTO BALLS, TASTE A LITTLE OF THE MIXTURE FOR SWEETNESS. IF YOU FIND IT IS NOT SWEET ENOUGH ADD A LITTLE MORE HONEY OR AGAVE SYRUP.

RAW CACAO, ORANGE AND COCONUT ROUGHS

MAKES 20—24

Soak the dates in hot water for 5 minutes to soften, then drain well.

In the meantime, place the almonds in a food processor and process until finely chopped.

Add the dates, cacao powder, orange zest and juice, coconut oil, maple syrup and coconut flakes to the food processor and process until the mixture comes together and you have a thick paste.

Wet the palms of your hands with cold water and roll the mixture into walnut-sized balls or whatever other size you prefer and then lightly coat in the extra coconut.

Refrigerate for at least 1-2 hours before serving.

Store in the refrigerator in a container with a lid, although I imagine there will not be many left to store.

5 oz/150 g Medjool dates, pitted
5 oz/150 g whole almonds
⅓ cup raw cacao powder
grated zest of 1 large orange
3 tablespoons orange juice
3 tablespoons melted organic raw coconut oil
2 teaspoons maple syrup
½ cup moist coconut flakes or shredded coconut
extra coconut, for coating

NOTE: BEFORE ROLLING INTO BALLS TASTE A LITTLE OF THE MIXTURE FOR SWEETNESS. IF YOU FIND IT IS NOT SWEET ENOUGH ADD A LITTLE HONEY OR AGAVE SYRUP.

RAW CHOCOLATE AND ORANGE MOUSSE

SERVES 2–4

½ cup raw cacao powder

½ cup coconut water

1 large ripe avocado, peeled and seed removed

2 teaspoons vanilla bean paste or extract

3 tablespoons honey or agave syrup

zest of 1 orange

1 tablespoon pure organic raw coconut oil

toasted almond flakes, crushed for garnish

fresh strawberries, for garnish

Mix the cacao powder and the coconut water together until you have a paste then place into the food processor with the avocado, vanilla, honey, orange zest and coconut oil.

Process until you have a very fine, soft and whipped mixture. You can process this mixture for quite a while in order to achieve a very fine and fluffy consistency. Don't worry about over-processing.

Keep in mind that the cacao powder is quite bitter so it is best to taste and adjust the level of sweetness to suit your taste.

Pour into individual dessert glasses or small coffee cups and refrigerate for about 2 hours before serving, topped with the toasted almonds and strawberries.

To toast the almond flakes, place the almonds into a small non-stick frying pan and lightly toast over a medium heat until golden, or roast in the oven.

NOTE: ALTHOUGH A HEALTHY DESERT, THIS IS STILL QUITE RICH SO YOU MAY WANT TO STRETCH THIS QUANTITY TO SERVE 4 PEOPLE AND SERVE IT IN SMALL COFFEE CUPS OR SHOT GLASSES. AS AN ALTERNATIVE, IF YOU LIKE GINGER, YOU CAN REPLACE THE ORANGE ZEST WITH GLACÉ GINGER.

RECIPE INDEX

ACKNOWLEDGEMENTS

I would like to thank my publisher Linda Williams and Fiona Schultz Managing Director of New Holland for giving me the opportunity to write this book and for their continued support and encouragement. This is our fifth cook book together and your belief in my work is very much appreciated and means so much.

A very special thank you, to my beautiful editor Jodi De Vantier for making the whole process of writing this book, our fourth together, so easy and for always being there for me. You are such a joy to work with.

A huge thank you, to my food stylist Tracy Rutherford and my photographer Sue Stubbs, for breathing life into my food. It has been such a pleasure to work with you both. You manage to make the long hard days of the photo shoot a breeze and such fun.

It has always been such a pleasure to work with all the team in New Holland, a huge thank you to all of you especially Tracy Loughlin, Diane Ward, Patsy Rowe, Lucia Donnelly and Natalie Christie for all your help and hard work throughout the whole process of publishing my books.

Lastly but by no means least, to my wonderful family, my husband Graeme, my children Alex, Nikki, and Christopher , their other halves Lachlan, Marcus and Carolyn, and to my gorgeous grandchildren Madison, Kobe and newest arrival Isaac and to my parents, thank you for your love, patience and understanding.